Shirdi Sai Baba
and other
Perfect Masters

Published by
Sterling Publishers Private Limited

SHIRDI SAI BABA
and other
PERFECT MASTERS

C. B. Satpathy

A Sterling Paperback

STERLING PAPERBACKS
An imprint of
Sterling Publishers (P) Ltd.
A-59 Okhla Industrial Area, Phase-II,
New Delhi-110020.
Tel : 6313023, 6320118, 6916165, 6916209
E-mail: ghai@nde.vsnl.net.in
www.sterlingpublishers.com

Shirdi Sai Baba and other Perfect Masters
© 2001, C. B. Satpathy
ISBN 81 207 2384 8
Reprint September 2001
Reprint 2003

Edited by Anandi Iyer
Published by Sterling Publishers Pvt. Ltd., New Delhi-110020.
Laserset at Vikas Compographics, New Delhi-110020.
Printed at Saras Graphics, Mayapuri, New Delhi.

Editor's Note

My fingers tremble as I muster courage to write this note. Can a speck of dust dream to describe the expanse of the *Perfect Masters*? Yet, my thoughts go back to the first day of my chance encounter with Shri C. B. Satpathy – Guruji or Baba, as he is fondly called by millions who have come into contact with him. Till that moment in time I was a hardcore professional, spiritual to the extent that one believes in the existence of a Superpower, yet firmly rooted in rationality and rational intelligence (!). In the instant when I connected with Shri Guruji's deep eyes, I was sent reeling into a hitherto unknown terrain – that of total surrender. In that one moment, it was as if I had met the source and final destination of my existence – and this ecstasy continues till date! This, then, is Sri C. B. Satpathy for the uninitiated.

For those who know him, the fact that he is divinity embodied does not come as a surprise at all. What inspires and stuns most is the *normalcy* with which he holds this divinity within him! He is foremost a family man, married with three children, and also a highly placed Government servant. Sai is the thread that weaves through every facet of his existence – be it through the soulful poems he writes, the spiritual heights he takes one to, through his melodious rendering of Sai bhajans, or the pun-filled humour that laces his speech. He is multi-talented, yet so down-to-earth that one who is not introduced to his versatility can hardly imagine it. His humility is amply reflected in the fact that he calls himself a servant of Sai Baba and implores Sai's followers to do the same.

His life is an inspiration, a lesson in sacrifice, healing and faith. Millions he has helped through service – be they lepers on the streets of Delhi, or those with worldly woes across the breadth of this country and beyond its shores. He has inspired countless people to tread along the path of Shri Sai and has been instrumental in building more than 50 temples of Shri Sai till date. Many more are in the pipeline, both nationally and internationally. He is a fatherly figure to those who meet him but once, and they remember him and feel his presence forever. His writings, in powerful English as well as in chaste Hindi, are timeless treasures, which one can hold on to while manoeuvring through the vicissitudes of life. Shri Satpathy has been writing small and big articles on Shirdi Sai since 1994 in different magazines both in Hindi and English. The idea of bringing those articles, his speeches delivered on different occasions rather extempore, in the form of a book was in fact a divine inspiration which I have dared to perform.

This book is a dedication to that moment, which gave many like me the strength and the *raison d'être* to live – that moment in which we met our beloved and revered Guruji.

Anandi Iyer

Contents

Contents

My Master

And I wake up suddenly from sleep
or wakefulness!
I do not know.

Ah ! there he was
his compassion unfathomable,
standing before me, in tattered clothes
and an unkempt beard,
with words that surpassed
a melodious symphony,
was I dreaming?
I do not know.

Then his glory in bright resplendent glow engulfed me,
his voice of divine ecstasy beholden -me, 'Child
I am your Master,
I am in you,
You came from me you came for me
that is your destiny awake and see,

The early morning's breeze
suddenly entered my room
his sweetened words entered my being,
At that moment I woke up
to know that forever, I belong to Him.

Some Revelations on the Sadgurus

T he *Sadguru* or Perfect Master or *Qutab* or Adept as he is called differently, is the pivotal point in the administration of the perceptible and the imperceptible universe around us. In fact the word *Qutab*, itself means pivot. Many visible and invisible activities stretching to aeons are conducted by these *Sadgurus* or Masters, working in unison with each other for the evolution of the living and non-living aspects of the universe. It is difficult to believe that the human civilisation on this earth of ours progressed exactly on the Darwinian presumptions of evolution. Modern historical research does not have the mechanism to delve into the vital role of these *Sadgurus* in changing the history of human society in all its aspects. Some historians have briefly touched upon this subject, but no one has really undertaken any serious research with this hypothesis or postulation, that behind every temporal ruler there is a spiritual ruler, or that all major changes in this world are programmed and executed by the *Sadgurus*, directly through the rulers and indirectly through certain unknown methods and spiritual workers. Therefore, historical research on the visible and invisible roles of the spiritual Masters or other spiritual personalities, working under the command of the *Sadgurus* in bringing about fundamental changes on the earth, is the need of the day. In rare cases, like the effect of *Sadguru* Ramdas on the Maratha rule of Shivaji in India, one gets a glimpse of the overt influence of a *Sadguru* on the political, social and moral life of a society. Similarly the effect and influence of Khwaja Moinuddin Chisti of Ajmer and of Nizamuddin Auliya of Delhi on the rulers of that time can be historically established. Even if a scholar has access to all the available historical data on the subject, a total comprehension of the role of these *Sadgurus* will elude him unless he has learnt about the secrets of spiritual science under the guidance of a *Sadguru*.

I have no doubt that in the case of every major and sudden happening on this earth, the causative force emanates from these spiritual leaders. They programme, motivate, organise and precipitate these happenings in order to bring in a new order by changing the old. Changing of societal or world orders can occur only when a mighty spiritual thrust is given by the spiritual Masters towards that direction. If Moses, Christ, Prophet Mohammed or Guru Nanak did not have the spiritual power with them, the changes they brought about and the religious orders they established would not have happened. Behind all such important happenings like wars, peace, change of rulers and forms of government, new discoveries and inventions in all fields of knowledge, particularly in all streams of science, their role can be seen. The unseen hands that write history are the hands of *Sadgurus*, the divine incarnates of the age. Shri Sai Baba of Shirdi used to say that Allah i.e. God has many officers all over. They are very powerful. Centuries ago, a Western philosopher Hegel, had made mention of the movement of what he called 'world spirit' or 'nature forces' in precipitating major incidents like wars. However, he did not spell out the mechanism by which, and the process through which such changes take place. Hindu spiritual science explains these aspects in detail, but they are known to a limited number of individuals on the spiritual path. Such knowledge is imparted by the *Sadgurus* to some deserving disciples only. The Masters are the precursors of the man of the fifth race that is yet to come. They have been carrying on this experiment on different planets, not only of our solar system but also on planets in other solar systems. The present research into the possible existence of organic life on heavenly bodies like Mars, Venus and the Moon in particular will be successful, as the Masters had earlier experimented on growth and sustenance of 'organic life forces' on these planets. Spiritual secrets revealed by the spiritual Masters indicate the generation of 'organic life forces' on earth by a spiritual entity called *Dakshya Prajapati*. Till one understands and realises the *Prajapati* concept, it will be treated as a mythological entity. It is believed that pre-birth and post-death conditions of all human souls have something to do with the Moon, the astral body nearest to the earth. These aspects cannot be discussed here, as the main issue is the role of the *Sadgurus* or Perfect Masters.

The *Sadgurus* are thus trying to advance evolution by raising the potential of man — the best of nature's creation on this planet. The blueprint of the future human civilisation is already with them, as a meticulously-drawn plan complete to the last detail within a perfect time scheme. As all the astral bodies like the milky ways, solar systems and planets have a certain periodicity of movement, changes in the solar systems and planets logically should follow certain time principles for the evolution of both organic and inorganic matter. The ancient Egyptians, the Kabala thinkers and the Chinese philosophers in the past attempted and somewhat succeeded in understanding these time-cycles of evolution. The ancient Hindu scriptures have dealt with the cycles of time to the last minute, not only with reference to the past, but also with reference to trillions of years ahead. Having full knowledge and command of the souls of all living beings, the *Sadgurus* play a vital role in drawing unto them all their devotees at the time of death and evolving their souls even in the post-death condition to higher levels of consciousness. They are the Perfect Masters, the perfect creatures of God anywhere in the universe. Their job is to bring perfection to anything and everything coming in contact with them, whether living or non-living, cutting across all reference of time, distance and space. Anyone coming into contact with them is bound to evolve whether he likes it or does not like it, whether it is to happen immediately or within a certain period of time. They are upholders of the ultimate laws of nature and the divine principles. They are not limited by human ego. They only work with a divine purpose. Their self is the divine self of God, radiating only compassion and creativity of the highest order. All deities and nature forces known as *devas* or *devis* in the Hindu pantheon assist them in the performance of their duties. Their wishes are the law of nature and God's command, even if invoked in the name of God. Shri Sai always used to invoke blessings saying *Allah malik hai* (God is the Lord of all) or *Ishwar Achcha Karega* (God will help).

However, they work mostly through a number of intermediary workers, who are spiritual personalities at different stages of evolution, both for training them and also for using them for specific jobs. These are addressed by different names as *Mahatma, Yogi, Muni, Sanyasi* in Hinduism and *Auliya, Pir, Mazoob or Kamil* by the Sufis. To realise God they have to go through many stages of evolution. After reaching the seventh stage of spiritual evolution they are known to be in a state of *Paramhamsa* or *Brahmistha* or *Brahmabhoot*. Once on this spiritual level, they are in the state of *Sat-Chit-Anand* i.e. God-State having His infinite power, knowledge and happiness. The spiritual powers in the other six stages carry out the work entrusted to them by the *Sadgurus* either directly or indirectly. Except for a few who are at a higher stage of evolution, most of these intermediary workers may not even know the source of their motivation, and of the energy they get to undertake such great tasks affecting the lives of hundreds and thousands of people. They work like possessed persons, under the mighty influence of the *Sadguru*. Many of them, when drawn by the Master, start behaving in a manner not experienced before and at times, they act in an unusual manner. Their internal thought process goes through a lot of change. The Master creates within them the qualities of love, sacrifice and forbearance. The entire personality of the disciple gets evolved in association with the *Sadguru*. History has shown that even the biggest sinners became saints in later life due to the play of *Guru Shakti* in them. This is what is called the 'Mercy of the Master' or *Guru Kripa*. They are the children of destiny working under the *Sadguru* and receive all their energy and powers from him. On the other hand the *Sadguru* becomes responsible for providing them with all the needs of life and also with protection. Some of these workers or disciples directly communicate with the *Sadguru* in his astral form. To thousands of people, they give direct help to facilitate evolution of their temporal and spiritual life. But for many more they work as invisible helpers, affecting them through their thought process. Lots of people get direction in dreams and others get unexpected help and direction, which logically cannot be explained. Due to their total attachment with the *Sadguru* their physical, astral and mental bodies also get linked with the physical, astral and mental bodies of the *Sadguru*. Their mutual bond of love is so strong that at times unknowingly, they start functioning in the same manner as their *Sadgurus*. These children of *Sadgurus*, who in Hinduism are known as *Ankita Santana* (i. e. children

earmarked to take over the role of the father at a later point
of time), when doing any work under the command of the
Guru or for his purpose, are endowed with the required powers
and energy to control all living forces, including human beings
and material forces. These are not their original powers, but
are powers delegated by the *Sadguru*. Their words of blessing,
invoked in the name of the *Sadguru*, can bring down an out
pouring of divine blessing from the *Sadguru*.

Some of them are so close to the *Sadguru* that even their
physical features replicate the physical features of the Master.
'The *Sadguru* blesses' means, he charges the devotee with some
amount of his spiritual power through the mediums of speech,
touch, look or even thought. The body, mind and astral body
of these workers are used by the *Sadguru* for radiating his
spiritual powers to other less-evolved disciples and devotees.
That is why in 1893 at Chicago and after Shri Paramahamsa
left his mortal body, Shri Vivekananda spread his message all
over and set up institutions to propagate Vedic knowledge all
over the globe. Having fulfilled the purpose of his divine
incarnation, Shri Vivekananda left his body at an early age,
just like Adi Shankara or Christ. Relating from the history of
Shirdi Sai, Shri Upasani Maharaj was drawn by Shri Sai with
a purpose. Shri Upasani Maharaj never knew that he was to
be the main disciple and 'charge man' of Shri Sainath. But
Shri Sai announced before everyone at Shirdi that He weighed
Shri Upasani Maharaj on one side and the whole world on
the other side of the spiritual scale. Such was the love of the
Sadguru that He took over the entire responsibility of Upasani
Maharaj, inspite of protests from and jealousy of many other
devotees, who thought that Upasani Maharaj did not deserve
all that attention from Shri Sai Baba. Shri Sai controlled the
life of Shri Upasani Maharaj so closely that when the latter
wanted to go back to his home, he was forced, under strange

circumstances to return to Shirdi within eight days, as Sai Baba had predicted. Similarly *Sadguru* Shri Lokanath Brahmachari of Baridi (now in Bangladesh) had drawn his main disciple Shri Bijay Krishna Goswami to himself by strange methods and evolved him to the state of a *Guru* in the late 19th century. The life histories of Sufi saints are full of such instances. These are only a few examples, but the *Sadgurus* always play the same or similar role with other disciples at various stages of development. These disciples, when evolved, also play the same or similar roles with their disciples. Thus the *Guru* lineage goes on and on. The inner motivation and methods of action of the disciple of the *Sadguru* cannot be completely understood by anybody other than the *Sadguru* who has taken over the entire responsibility of such a devotee. All other persons, including his family members and closest relatives cannot understand the value of this disciple. The world may or may not be able to recognise his inner virtues and may even discard him, but the *Sadguru* who is the *Antar-Sakshi*, (the witness of his inner self), always loves him and stands by him. Gradually this disciple comes to realise the limitations of human love and the illusions of worldly games, and totally surrenders to his *Guru* — the spring of eternal love. He has no choice, once he is chosen by the *Sadguru*.

In the *Autobiography of a Yogi*, written by Shri Yoganand, it is mentioned that the disciple Shri Lahiri Mahashaya and his *Guru* Shri Mahavatara Baba had striking physical similarities. In some cases, even the voice and way of expression of the *Sadguru* and his close disciple have been found to be similar. The *Sadguru*, the pivot of the universe ushers in all major and important events of history like change of rulers, wars, large-scale destructions, new discoveries that lead human civilisation forward in the path of evolution, spread and sustenance of spiritual energy on earth through temples, churches and other groups carrying on such missions. Only a few evolved souls can know as to which Master, through what method has precipitated wars, brought about peace and opened the door to new fields of knowledge to help mankind. In the 21st century, the play of the divine power will be manifesting progressively on a vaster scale and at a greater speed, as the complexities of human civilisation are on the increase. The fourth human race has crossed half-way in its evolution. Now the *Sadgurus* or the Perfect Masters are extremely busy in evolving the human capacity to higher potentials and magnitudes to bring in the fifth human race with much superior potential. The exploration of space, genetic engineering, discovery of sub-particles of the atom, unbelievable expansion of information technology, oceanic explorations, cloning of animals, spread of occultism and paranormal experiments are indications in that direction. Today communication takes place through the medium of electromagnetic waves. Tomorrow, the fifth human race will develop the capacity to communicate through a mental process with each other. Newer and newer energy fields will be discovered and used by human beings. The ancient knowledge of *Vedas*, *Yoga*, Pyramids, Astrology, *Vaastu* and Parapsychological experiments will be rediscovered. These fields of knowledge have not been given for the first time to the human race on this earth. They had been imparted to earlier civilisations and in different planets and universes. The information of every thing of the past is in the sky in a subtle energy form. Only a few can explore and access it.

Today human civilisation is on the threshold of a change. These Masters at different points of history and in different parts of the world had given thrust and evolved human civilisations in the past. Among these were the Sumerian,

Atlantis, Egyptian, Roman, Aztec, Peruvian, Harappan, Aryan and Chinese civilisations. During this century many lost civilisations will be discovered, some of which are hidden under the seas. In the history of time, the past re-enacts as the present just as the present contains the past. Even in ancient times the *Sadgurus* came on this earth as the Hindu *rishis* like Kapila, Vasistha, Suka, Vishwamitra, Bharadwaj and Dattatreya. In other countries they came as Herrnes, Enoch, Orpheus and others. They reincarnated as Abraham, Zoroaster, Moses, Buddha, Christ, Prophet Mohammad, Adi Shankara and many others in different countries and at different times. These sons of God the Almighty, born in groups in different parts of human society, taught the human race at its infant state its primary lessons in science and arts and gave a thrust to the progress of human civilisation. They descended on the Egyptian civilisation and taught them Occult sciences, building of Pyramids, Geometry, Alchemy, etc. Earlier they had built the Atlantis civilisation, the mother of the later civilisations, which has drowned in the sea. They taught Architecture, Design, Mathematics, principles of warfare, etc. to the mighty Roman Empire. They built the Mohenjodaro civilisation and the Aryan civilisation and gave the Vedic knowledge to posterity. When any of these most compassionate beings descends on earth in human form, all the *Yogis* and saints come to know about it through their *yogic* (divine) perception; it is for His arrival that they have been praying for many lives. When a large number of human beings suffer on earth due to tyranny or misrule (*Adharma* as the Hindus call it), their prayers to the Almighty force the all-powerful divine power to descend in human form and stabilise the forces of nature (that is, establish *Dharma*). All the forces of nature mirthfully welcome His coming. When Lord Krishna was born, the saints knew that the suffering souls would be redeemed and liberated, as the *Narayan Shakti* (highest divine power) had descended. When Jesus was born, the three wise men from the East, i.e. the three spiritual souls from India knew and reached Bethlehem following the star that guided them. When Lord Buddha, having attained Nirvana, returned to the world to relieve the suffering humanity of their pain and bondage, nature became joyous. It is thus explained in the book titled *Voice of the Silence* : "all Nature thrills with joyous awe and feels subdued. The silver star now twinkles out the news to the night blossoms, the streamlet to the pebbles ripples out the tales; dark ocean waves will roar it to the rocks surf-bound, scent-laden breezes sing to its vales and stately pines mysteriously whisper — A Master has arisen, a Master of the Day."

A pilgrim has returned from the other shore. Yes, the Masters are coming from that shore, from the abode of the Gods, out of their infinite compassion for all of us. The forces of nature on this good earth of ours have started vibrating and tuning themselves for the advent of these mighty divine powers. Some of them are already born and working in a quiet manner in different corners of the earth. Their workers and disciples at various stages of spiritual evolution are also getting ready to welcome them. These disciples in different places of the world are continuously praying for their early advent. After all, during the last century the earth experienced two devastating wars. The world today is going through a process of 'intellect explosion' in all fields of knowledge. Yet the lack of moral values to properly utilise the fruits of the intellect for the greatest good of the greatest number on this earth is the biggest limitation. It is these Masters who will redefine religious codes and re-establish moral values on earth. Human beings in future will certainly communicate through mental processes and discover those powers which today are known as the occult powers of *Siddhis. Siddhi* (occult power) is nothing but a principle of nature yet undiscovered by the present human race. When the Masters will teach the principles of governing these unexplored laws of nature, new vistas of knowledge will open up before the human race. The *Sadgurus* of the present age are active and are carrying on the administration of the universe as before. They are assisted by a number of spiritual workers functioning at different parts of the world. Until they reveal themselves, no one can really know who they are and cannot have an idea about their activities. When the time comes, they will reveal themselves and the whole world will come to recognise these *Sadgurus* and shall surrender to them. We can only pray to Shri Sai Baba of Shirdi, the 'Incarnation of the Age' to reveal the divine mystery to us. We appeal to these magnificent and divine beings to bless us.

Shri Shirdi Sai Baba

Shirdi Sai Baba

1838	Born in a Brahmin family in Maharashtra.
1842 – 1854	He was with His Guru known as "Venkusha".
1854	Materialised under a neem tree in Shirdi.
1857	Left Shirdi.
1858	Returned to Shirdi.
1885	Left His body for 3 days and came back to life.
1897	Initiation of Urs fair and the Sandal Procession.
1912	Transformation of Urs into Ramnavami Festival.
1912	Installation of Padukas under the Neem tree.
1916	Seemollangan. Gave an indication of His passing away on Vijayadashmi day.
1918, Oct 15	Attains Mahasamadhi on Vijayadashmi Day.

Shri Sai Baba of Shirdi:
An Incarnation

I ndian sub-continent was the abode of great saints and seers during the nineteenth and the first half of the twentieth century. The last century witnessed the emergence of divine personalities like Shri Ramakrishna Paramahamsa, Shri Nigamananda, Shri Lahiri Mahasaya, Shri Lokanath Brahmachari, Shri Bamakshepa, Shri Vivekananda and Shri Bisudhananda Saraswati, etc., in the north-eastern belt of India. More specifically they were confined to the adjacent areas of rivers like the Ganges, the Yamuna and the Brahmaputra. Indians are well aware of the divine qualities of these enlightened souls. During that period there also took place the divine manifestations of the seers of Western and Central India, who used to stay on the basins of great rivers like the Narmada and the Godavari. But in reality, the seers who have realised the absolute or have reached the highest realm of spiritual attainment are present forever in the whole universe, whether in an embodied or in an unembodied state. They can operate in the gross, subtle or mental world. By virtue of their divine powers they touch upon both the animate and the inanimate world. They have been defined by different names like Brahmishta, Paramahamsa or Jeevan-mukta, etc., and are free from the chains of life and death. They are in a sublime state of *Turiya* or have gone beyond it. They have been actually chosen to execute the divine mission and for that, all categories of these seers, free from individual ego, work together for the execution of the divine mission. Some of the seers stay away from the crowd and employ their spiritual powers from a secluded corner for the deliverance of the people. This is one of the manifestations of their spirit of compassion. They are, indeed, the ambassadors of divine compassion. A few of them, due to this compassion for humanity are embodied in the world to uplift the souls of the fallen and the suffering. They are revered as *Sadgurus* or perfect masters by the scriptures.

Five *Sadgurus* are said to operate in the whole world in a particular milieu and one of them is indeed, a *Param Sadguru*. They are assisted by 51 spiritually-realised *Sidhas*, both corporeal and non-corporeal. Besides this, in this hierarchy there are about 5000 evolved souls stationed on different rungs in the ladder of spiritual enlightenment. This galaxy of seers is said to be functional or operative for a period of about or more. These are spiritual secrets of the highest under seven hundred years.

The seers who mainly resided on the banks of the rivers Godavari and Narmada in the 19th and the first half of the 20th century were Shri Akkalkot Maharaj (Maharashtra), Shri Tazuddin Baba (Nagpur, Madhya Pradesh), Shri Gajanan Avadhoot (Seogam, Maharashtra), Shri Baba Jan and Shri Sankar Maharaj (Pune, Maharashtra), Shri Meher Baba (Ahmednagar), Shri Narayani Maharaj (Sakuri, Maharashtra), Shri Narayani Maharaj (Khed Gaon, Maharashtra) and above all Shri Shirdi Sai Baba (Shirdi, Maharashtra).

Shri Shirdi Sai Baba, who flourished in the later half of the 19th century, remains as a the *Param-Sadguru* for the coming seven centuries even after leaving his mortal body, as devotees experience today. The *Sadgurus*, transcending all the confines of caste, sect and colour, remain engaged in the spiritual up lift of humanity and operate on both the physical and metaphysical planes. Even animals, birds and other living creatures are treated compassionately by them. The lifestyle of Sai Baba and his routine functioning reflected that he was full of compassion for the redemption of the people. His place of abode was accessible to all and sundry. While in Shirdi he was occupying Dwarakamayee, a dilapidated mosque, and was venerated both by the Hindus and the Muslims according to their respective customs. During his lifetime, both the Hindus and Muslims used to celebrate various festivals jointly. The tombs of his close initiates like Abdul Baba and Tatiyakote Patil are found around the same place at Shirdi. The consecrated flame which was lit by the holy Sainath at Shirdi, still continues to burn. Fire-worship is one of the important sacraments of the Zoroastrians. It is surprising that a large number of Parsees in India happen to be followers of Shirdi Sai Baba. The Holy Sainath, though dressed like a Muslim, had his earlobes perforated, the system which is in vogue in the Natha tradition. It is needless to reiterate that the country has been favoured with Matsyendra Nath, Gorakh Nath, etc. the *Param-Yogins* of the Natha tradition. Ashes collected from the sacred flame lit by Baba have been efficacious in relieving people from various diseases and mundane afflictions. Baba always preferred the company of his followers and shunned luxurious living. He use to lie on a torn rag and rest his head on a piece of brick. Among his personal belongings, he had a chillam, a *satka* (stick) and his torn *kufni*. He use to mend his own cloth. Sometimes, he gave away to the Dhuni, garments that he had worn only once. The foodstuffs offered to him on silver platters by his rich devotees used to be distributed amongst the poor. Thousands of rupees given to him every day as *dakshina* were also distributed on the same day by him. Every day he would have amassed a royal sum and by night he would again be a pauper. The day when he left his mortal body he had only nine coins at his disposal, which he gifted away to one of his devotees as a token of blessing. This is verily in keeping with the scriptural description of Lord Shiva. Baba was a Shivatma.

Today, when India and the whole world is torn asunder with religious conflicts, communal strife and armed clashes, the stream of compassion of the great humanist Shri Sainath is yet flowing unabatedly. Today Shirdi is being visited by around 30 thousand people every day on an average for paying homage to the Shrine of Baba, and their number is increasing everyday. The semi-government organisation, Sai-Sansthan of Shirdi is struggling to take care of the ever-increasing number of pilgrims. Many temples are being constructed both in India and abroad dedicated to Shirdi Sai. Reports about the construction of temples in honour of Sainath have been reaching every week. In Andhra Pradesh alone there exist as many as 250 major Sai temples. Thousands of people have been inspired to build temples on their own and have been preaching the Sai philosophy here and abroad. The growing multitude of Sai devotees signals that the historic Sai movement would establish in the coming century, 'peace and amity' in India and abroad. Shri Sai is the incarnation of the age and therefore faith in Him is bound to spread with far-reaching consequences in the future. Only time will prove this.

What Baba Looked Like

T he incarnations and saints usually have certain physical features. These have been described in different books written on the saints. Shri Sai Baba of Shirdi had some special features:

Shri Sainath was of the height of about 5 feet 8 inches or so, given the length of *Kafni* he was wearing. A comparison of Baba's height with that of the other devotees' photographed with Him in standing position is also an indicator.

He had a lean and flexible body and used to walk in a sportsman-like manner in His young days. His famous wrestling bout at Shirdi in His earlier days is indicative of His stamina and well-developed muscles. The colour of His body was very fair at the initial stage with a light orange hue. There was an attractive glow on His skin.

Baba's hands and legs were longer than His torso. His palm along with fingers and feet were oversized, as may be seen in His photographs. This can be further established from His footwear now preserved by the Shirdi Sai Sansthan at Shirdi.

In His young age Baba had curly hair on the head but later became bald on the top leaving a scanty ring of hair around. Because He wore a headgear, except when He took a bath, it was not noticeable.

He had long ears and they were perforated. His eyes were deep-seated and the eyeballs had a bluish tinge. His looks were focussed and highly penetrative, as if He could see through the man before Him. He sported a moustache and kept a thin beard, which used to be trimmed regularly by the local barber. He had prominent forehead lines, above the nose ridge. His lips were thick and full. By old age he had lost many of His teeth and at times used to gulp down food.

This then was Shirdi Sai the Perfect Master, with all the physical indicators of a divine soul as have been described in the scriptures – i.e. long arms and legs (*Ajanubahu*), long ears (*Sukarna*) glow in the skin (*Divya Kanti*), focussed and penetrative looks (*Sthira Drishti*), etc.

Sai Comes To My Life

To write a book on Shri Shirdi Sai had nowhere been in my thoughts, four years ago. Today, I can think of writing on nothing else, but His glory. I always question myself as to why this situation should have arisen in my life. Whatever I think, whatever I do in the mundane or on a purely mental plane, His thoughts appear quietly in the background of my mind. He appears sitting on a stone, His right leg over the left, looking upwards with all His glory in that tattered *kafni* that He perennially donned. His white headgear would be shining bright in His splendour. This image would remain for long, disturbing my worldly routine. Howsoever I would like to separate my consciousness from it, His thoughts would not leave me, all-pervasive and all-blissful. I would feel restless like a fish in the fisherman's net, not being able to cope with the conflicting demands of family, job, relatives and social life. Willy-nilly, pushing His thoughts to the background I would take out my car, go to the market with the family to purchase household requirements, to give them an occasional cold drink and purse permitting, even a pastry. In the market, or while sitting in the car, I would often be the victim of a familiar trick played on me. I would suddenly notice a photograph of Shri Sainath in a shop, or a locket with His photo on some lady's neck, or even a ring on somebody's finger. My first reaction would be to avoid looking at it by concentrating on the display items of the shop, or on the people walking around. I would even try to get away mentally to distant places like London and Tokyo, which I had once seen, with the earnest hope that at least in these places, there would be nothing akin to India, thereby reducing the probability of thoughts of Shri Sainath entering my mind. I would think about the palace of the King of Japan. I would concentrate on the beautiful lake garden at Tokyo, where in the eerie silence of a departing day, I had seen an old man sitting on a bench, feeding the ducks. The moment this old man's picture with a white cap and beard would cross my mind, trouble would start afresh. His picture would transform in my mind to that of Shri Sainath. I would get a jerk. He would seem to laugh. How far I had flown in His thought, almost like a lover's dream.

Such unsolicited mental union became a part of my existence, day and night, not leaving me alone even during sleep. Normally, one devotes a major part of one's waking hours to mundane pursuits of life, except, perhaps, when one is in 'love'. My plight is that normally I think about Shri Sai and only occasionally, about other activities. For one who is afflicted with such love, the worldly activities gradually shrink to a minimum, leaving more and more time for Him. The moment I would get into my bed, His thoughts would play hide-and-seek with me. In those tranquil moments, He would appear in my mind in almost a three-dimensional image and then suddenly disappear. I would try to catch Him again. This 'transformation' in my life has surprised me, no less than my family members and close friends. All the familiar terms like birth, death, world, nature, religion, cosmos, etc. have suddenly acquired a new meaning. My attempts to consciously swim against this 'time-flow of a mighty force beyond comprehension,' have failed. The more I resisted, the less I understood its meaning. I knew the force when I surrendered. It is Shri Sainath and His Grace. It always hovers there, inseparable and inalienable. I bask in His Glory; I delight in His splendour, yet am never content.

How did it happen? Did I try for it? Did I pray for Him? Did I practise *Hatha Yoga* or *Raja Yoga* to attract His attention? None of those normal methods of propitiation of deities was performed by me. Till 1989, I did not know anything about Shri Shirdi Sai except that I had heard His name in the context of Shri Satya Sai Baba. Yet His Grace had so suddenly devolved on me, in a most unexpected way!

It had happened suddenly. There is a video shop in Palika Bazaar near my house, from where I used to occasionally collect video cassettes. I do not remember the exact date, but it was sometime in November 1989. I went to the shop to collect a certain film cassette. It was not available. I scanned most of the cassettes, but none was appealing. Suddenly I saw a cassette on Shirdi Sai Baba produced by Manoj Kumar. I enquired about the cassette from the owner, who told me that children love it for the many miracles of Shirdi Sai Baba that have been shown therein. The word 'miracle' also stimulated some interest in me. I had always been fond of seeing films about the supernatural and had read books on the subject.

Miracles I had seen during my childhood. I hail from a place called Baripada, a district town in Orissa. It is situated in a tribal belt, replete with hills and thick luxuriant rain forests inhabited by elephants, deer, bears and other wild animals. The tribals with whom our family has been intimately connected for generations, and who continue to cultivate our hereditary lands, are known to practise black magic. It is some what similar to Voodoo practice in Africa. They can put a snake to sleep, set a place on fire, stop a cow from giving milk or even kill it, dry up a tree, etc. I have seen persons affected by tribal occultism. In my early childhood my father was

posted in a place called Berhampur, adjacent to the tribal belt
in South Orissa. It must have been sometime in 1956, when
I was a child, that I saw two miracles. I saw a person giving a
show in a public place near the railway station. He placed a
thick coiled rope on the ground. He uttered something and
threw some dust on the rope. Suddenly one end of the rope
started moving up towards the sky slowly. After a few minutes,
the whole rope stood erect at a height of about twelve to fifteen
feet. Later I came to know that it had been the famous Indian
'rope trick.'

Whether it was black magic or a mere trick, I cannot
vouchsafe, as I was too young then. However, all the people
who saw it praised him and donated a lot of money. The other
miracle I saw was a bout between two persons practising black
magic. This again, I saw at Berhampur around the same time.
Both the persons sat apart on the ground at a distance, facing
each other. They wore only a dhoti in a peculiar manner. The
upper part of the body was naked. They indulged in attacks
and counter-attacks using magical powers as their weapons.
Towards the end, one of them took a bamboo pole and fixed
its lower portion into the ground. The bamboo stood about
four to five feet above the ground. He smeared it with some
liquid. Then he chanted some mantras and lashed the bamboo
pole with a whip. His adversary sitting at a distance, suddenly
jumped up in excruciating pain and fell panting on the ground.
The other person whipped the bamboo pole three or four
times more. Each time he did so, the victim cried out in pain.
At last he surrendered himself to his adversary. While he lay
prostrate in agony, I could clearly see his back. It had three or
four clear lacerated wounds, as if he had been actually whipped.
Blood oozed out of these wounds profusely. I was scared and
ran back home. When I narrated this to my mother, she
forbade me to visit such places again.

I had read a number of books about saints and miracle-men in my early childhood. I knew that Swami Vivekananda saw a different Universe than is ordinarily visible, when Ramakrishna Paramahamsa touched him. I read that Moses had made the sea part to allow safe passage to the fleeing children of Israel. I knew that some saints could even know the time of their own death. They entered *samadhi* at a pre-ordained time. But this understanding had been purely on an intellectual plane. Therefore, when I heard about the miracles of Shri Sai Baba of Shirdi, I decided to see the film. Little did I know at that point of time, that yet another miracle was about to take place. My life would stand transformed in a matter of a few hours.

At home I played the cassette after lunch. The first few episodes were full of miracles like curing people and turning water into oil, defying all reason. The early miracles of Shri Sai Baba were soon over. Then the later episodes were shown. When Shri Sai Baba was shown in a *samadhi* state for 72 hours, I had a strange feeling. Initially I could not believe my eyes. The image of Shri Sai Baba in His old age would suddenly vanish and my father's image would appear in its place. My father, the only person in whom all my love had been concentrated, had departed for his heavenly abode as far back as 1982. No one had been able to take his place. At first, I thought it was a projection of my own thoughts. I turned my gaze away from the television screen towards the sky and the trees that I could see through the window. Then, I focused my sight on the screen again. Shri Sainath was still in *samadhi* and the devotees were praying to Him to regain His consciousness. Again the image changed to that of my father. I switched off the television when this happened once more. Nonetheless, I tried to reason it out. I put my lifetime experience and knowledge to the test. Could it be that I had been longing for my father? Could it be that the appearances of my father and that of Shri Sainath were alike? However, they did not match at all. Shri Sainath was a tall person, about 6 feet in height. My father had been of medium height, about 5'-6". The face of Shri Sainath was long, He had a beard and the looks of a Muslim fakir. My father's face had been round and I had never seen him with a beard.

The next morning we left for Shirdi, promptly at 5.30 a.m. We had breakfast at Nasik. We also found some time to make a visit to the Muktidham, a huge temple complex with accommodation for about 200 pilgrims. On my way to Nasik from Bombay, I had been lost in my own thoughts. I was contemplating the manner in which I was being literally dragged to appear before Him at Shirdi. I had read about the call of the spiritual Masters to their devotees. I knew the Great Masters keep watch over their disciples, life after life, through the eternal cycle of life and death. They guard their devotees from the stage of 'infants within the mother's womb' to death and thereafter. The disciples are fished out of this material world for the fulfilment of their true mission at a propitious moment, for which they are made ready through a series of pains and pleasures. Had there been such a call from Shri Sai or is it coincidental, I thought. How was I to know? Had there been a Sign? The only Sign had been that I was undertaking this journey unexpectedly and in an unplanned manner, and stood in imminent danger of missing my flight back to Delhi in the event of even a minor mishap. This did not appear as a pleasant prospect to me, not then.

I prayed for a clear Sign. I challenged Him, mentally of course. If He was my Guru and was calling me, I should be able to garland His statue at Shirdi. I enquired from my host if it would be possible. I was informed that since the queue at Shirdi was likely to be long, it would not be possible to do so.

For the first time in my life I prayed for a small favour to Him — to accept my garland.

At Muktidham we worshipped the various deities including Shri Ram-Sita, Radha-Krishna, Shivji, etc. Suddenly Shri Sainath in white marble sitting with right leg over the left engaged my attention. I had never expected to find Him so suddenly in this temple. *Aarti* was in progress. We procured garlands and stood behind the crowd, waiting for an opportunity to creep closer for a better view. I was holding a big garland in my hand. The *aarti* was concluded within a short time and the crowd surged forward in expectation of *prasad*. Suddenly the priest looked at me and asked for my garland. He beckoned me to come nearer and to put the garland I had been carrying on the statue of Shri Sai. I did so, rather elated. I noticed to my great surprise, that while garlands offered by others had been put around the neck of the statue, only to be taken off, my garland remained. I was thrilled with joy. Yet the doubt remained whether it was sheer coincidence or a divine indicator.

From His side Shri Sai had spoken. The message beat into my head loud and clear that my search had ended. This was the Call that I had waited for, from the first breath of my life. I had always felt an unknown pain of wanting something in life which I was not able to identify. The pain of a meaningless existence had been gnawing at my heart. It had been my constant companion ever since my birth. I had known all along without anyone telling me, that this had been the pain of 'separation'. This separation was the central theme of Sufism, about which I had read. Even the Bhakti cult was based upon the longing of the *bhakt* for his God, whom he saw with the eyes of a lover. Poetry spouts from the lover's heart for his Beloved, creating a universe within. It is a universe of 'intense love'. It is a different thing to understand this in an intellectual sense. But now suddenly the doors of this universe had been thrown open to me. I plunged into a state of pure ecstasy, savouring its delight within me, till I was at one with it. All perceptions of space and time vanished. It was joy and 'pure joy' all the way to Shirdi.

My inner self said it was His indication, but the intellect continued to play its tricks, doubting and questioning. In any case, upto Shirdi I was in a mood of ecstatic expectation.

We reached Shirdi around mid-noon. We purchased *naivedya* and flowers for offering and took our place at the end of the serpentine line which snaked its way through the temple right upto Him. My host informed me that we were lucky to be here on a Thursday, an auspicious day for the worship of the Baba, the *Param Sadguru*. I had been lucky, I thought to myself, to have reached Him on His day. Was it pre-ordained or it was just coincidental? Did He want me to come on a Thursday? The queue had not moved even an inch forward, I noticed , within half an hour. My thoughts turned back to my flight, which I was now bound to miss. At this rate we may not be able to reach Baba even by four in the afternoon. There was nothing else to do except to pray. I prayed to Him fervently, standing in the queue. Minutes later I heard a person call me by my name. I could not recognise him. He knew me as we had met in Delhi earlier. I, of course, could not remember this. Seeing our plight, he offered to make arrangements for an early *darshan*. He left, to return in a few minutes with the good news.

We were led through an adjoining room to the *samadhi*. Baba's statue was there as if in flesh and blood, splendid in the ochre robes. Before I could concentrate on His face or on the *samadhi*, the queue moved forward. The crowd continued to jostle from behind. But then, even a moment had been enough. One look at His face filled me with a strange joy I had never known before. His face was so sublime and so familiar, as if an old memory of a childhood friend had suddenly come back to life. I hurtled back some seventy-two years in time. I was back to the Shirdi Baba's days. He was the same and very much there. Divine glory poured forth from His face, from every pore of His body. He appeared to gaze at me. There was a hint of a smile at the corner of His lips. What is happening to you, I asked myself? The inner voice echoed – this is the moment for which you have been waiting since your birth. A strange sense of separation and also reunion swept over me like giant tidal waves in succession. Everything felt so divine. Those few moments were more intoxicating than all the liquor in the world.

I hardly possessed the sense to notice that the priest had taken the flowers from us and made offerings to the *samadhi*. Again, my garland adorned the Sai. This time the sign was clearer. The queue moved again and we found ourselves outside the temple near the Gurusthan under the neem tree. We moved from the Gurusthan to the Dwarkamayee and then to the Chawdi and the Khandoba temple. By the time we finished, it was past two in the afternoon. All of us were hungry. I thought in my mind that I would be happy to get a little *kheer* in a container, as I had been told that it would be available in *prasad* on Thursday. My host and his namesake Vijay went to the *langar* for arranging a meal, where thousands were lined up before us. They came back to report that the food counter had closed. No food from the Shirdi temple, it was fine, I thought. Food could be taken from the hotels. But denial of a little *kheer* as *prasad* really hurt me. Did not Baba know that I just wanted a little *prasad* out of love? I sat down under a tree and continued to pray. My host and Vijay went out again to return a few minutes later, with the news that lunch would be served to us in the VIP room. Even though I was doubtful, they assured me that they had made all arrangements for lunch. I followed them to the kitchen block and then to the VIP dining room. We sat waiting anxiously for lunch to be served. Utensils were placed on the table in front of us.

It was then that a strange thing happened. One of the organisers, who had promised that lunch was on its way, suddenly started apologising as food items had been exhausted. However, there was some *kheer* left which he could manage for us. It was brought some ten minutes later. I could recognise the container immediately, as I had imagined and prayed for it. This could be no coincident I thought. It was His Grace. I was moved intensely. He had millions of people and the whole universe to look after. Yet He was so concerned with the small desire of a humble creation like me. Was I so important to Him? Or was He so merciful to me? I knew it was His mercy. My tears flowed for a long time. Once they had ceased, everything had changed. I felt I had met my Spiritual Master, my long-lost Guru. It was not He who had been lost. It was I, who like a vagrant child had wandered here and there, after material pursuits. He had found me out and had called me back home. My friends were surprised to find me in this state, for they did not know what I was thinking. I was in my own world.

The journey back to Delhi was the beginning of my journey on the path of Sai. I started meditating on His form for hours during the night and even during the day. I read most of the books written on Him in English and in Hindi. I had searched through books on spiritualism, the occult and religion. I had read to find out if there was anything written on Him. I read Swami Muktanand's *Chitsakti Vilas* and found that in his state of *samadhi*, he had seen Shri Sainath in *Sidhaloka* (the abode of the Adepts). I read the books of Avtar

Meher Baba. He had clearly said, "If you know Him as I know Him, you would call Him the master of creation." I went through the lives of Kabir, Sarmad, Tukaram, Sant Gyaneshwar, Namdev, Tulsi, Hathras, Bulleh Shah, Nanak and other saints, published by the Radha Swami organisation. I tried to learn about the path of the *Sidhas*, the mystics and the Sufi saints. All my intellectual wanderings ended in one clear conclusion. Shri Sainath personifies the quintessence of all scriptures and paths. I had imperceptibly crossed the barriers of the limited mind and moved from doubt and confusion to conviction and faith. I realised that even if He has cast off His mortal body, He remains as He had always been. He had played one role in the human garb. He plays another without it.

I continuously chanted His Mantra "Om Shri Sai Nathaya Namah." I started visiting His temple at Lodhi Complex, Delhi regularly thereafter. Since 1986 I had been meeting hundreds of people every Saturday, who used to come to me for astrological predictions and other consultations. By the year 1990 this number had multiplied to more than a thousand a month. There was so much of suffering around. The want was frightening. It was not always need-based. It was greed that compelled some of the people to undertake various material pursuits, often with dubious intent and methods. No science, no medicine, no intellectual advice can solve the problem of the *homo-sapiens*. Then what could I do when people came to meet me with expectations? Where is the universal healer for all the ills of the world? The name of Sai was the only medicine that I could prescribe. I had even made experiments on ailing persons suffering with diseases like hypertension, epilepsy, etc. I had built a pyramid at my residence and had studied its effect on various functions of the body earlier. But *Sainaam* was the best method, as I visualised.

Continuous meditation on Shri Sainath introduced me
to a strange world rather imperceptibly. The devotees of Shri
Shirdi Sai gradually began to gather around me. Some of them
had not even known that I was also one of His devotees. One
day a person named Raju met me to say that he had been
directed in a dream to see me. The same thing happened to
one Gulati. Soon more people from Delhi and other parts of
India came, obeying some mysterious command, because of
which they came to meet me. I always discouraged them, as I
continue to do today, saying that such experiences are often
aberrations of the mind and are coincidental by nature. They
have little to do with mystical experiences. The more I denied,
the more people started approaching me with such mystical
commands. At times they even thought that I had some
mystical powers. I refused to meet such people, and
deliberately ignored them with the earnest hope that some
sanity would prevail in them and in me. I even tried to convince
them that I was an ordinary person having a family and doing
a job to eke out my livelihood. I suffer from all the sordid
problems of the mundane world like disease, want, anger and
problems with the boss in the office. Having gone through so
many books on the subject, I had an intellectual understanding
about such phenomena. But to understand something
academically is different from actually undergoing the
experience. Although I rejected these incidents as mere
coincidence, their number started increasing further. One day
a Mrs. Joshi rang up from London, saying that she had been
suffering from a physical problem and the doctors have not
been able to help her. I told her that I could only try to help if
she came to Delhi. She replied that her condition was such
that she could only be carried to India on a stretcher. I heard
a voice command within me, "Then let her come on a
stretcher." She came to India on a Saturday and waited for

me in a queue in front of my house for about eight hours
without any problems. I gave her *bibhuti* (sacred ash) of Baba
and taught her how to worship Him. Her relief from pain
was instantaneous. She visited India again in July - August,
1993. She made her obeisance to Shri Sai at Shirdi. She is
one of His devotees now. Sai has given a new life to her.

The case of a property dealer in Delhi was still more
strange. One day his three minor sons disappeared, leaving
behind a note that they were tired of the matrimonial discord
between their parents. The couple searched for them
frantically. Even police help was taken, but to no avail. The
children seemed to have disappeared without a trace. Broken
in spirit and desperate, the father approached me on a
Saturday. Having listened to his problem, I prayed to Shri
Sainath for help. Suddenly it flashed in my mind that his
children were safe and would return soon. I had a vision that
one of them had developed a limp. I could also see that the
couple was destined for some more suffering. One must reap
the consequences of one's acts, not only in the lives to follow,
but also in this very lifetime. This is what Shri Sai had said.
Sai is all compassion. I knew that particularly for the penitent,
expression of remorse is a step towards Sai. Whenever
someone takes one small step towards Sai, He takes ten steps
towards him/her. I was moved by the tears flowing down the
cheeks of the lady. I directed the couple to immediately visit
the Sai Temple at Lodhi Complex and worship Baba, after
having presented him a yellow *chadar* and a coconut. It is not
that Baba has any need of these articles. It only symbolises
a feeling which the devotee has for Sai. We prayed to Baba
for his children.

The couple did exactly as had been required of them. Lo
and behold, within two days there was a telephone call
from Patna informing them that the boys had reached there

and also that one boy had injured his leg. Ever since then, the family has been worshipping Baba.

Hundreds of incidents of this type started happening around me. The crowd, seeking my intervention in their personal matters, started multiplying. I started receiving letters from all over the country and abroad, from people I had never known and who belonged to different strata and communities. I had only one panacea to prescribe for all their maladies. Sai was the 'Giver'. One needs only to pray to Him. We dispatched photographs of Sai and a little bit of the *udi (bibhuti)*. Even my family members were not untouched. They began to have a series of experiences, miraculous in nature. Responses to the photographs of Sai, which we had sent earlier, began to pour in. People started writing about their experiences with Shri Sainath once they had started worshipping His photo and using His *bibhuti*. It was astounding. It was amazing. Sai's name was a miracle in itself – a cure for all ailments of the body and life.

How could so many coincidences take place together? Had I a spiritual preceptor, I would have surely asked him to explain. Unfortunately my Guru, my Guide, my Sainath had entered his *Mahasamadhi* in the year 1918, decades before I was born. I can only ask Him to give me the answers in His own way.

I went through the books of Mehar Baba and Upasani Maharaj, as they had been close disciples of Shri Sai and had received spiritual sustenance from him. I started meditating on Him for an answer. In the meantime, the people had started meeting me in large numbers. The press also became interested in me and started collecting material, mainly through interviews of persons who had been beneficiaries. Some of them wrote long articles. The crowd at my residence swelled further. Many important personalities, including businessmen, politicians and administrative officers began to approach me with the hope that I had a panacea for all their material problems. Even people practising Yoga, *Pranayam*, Meditation and other spiritual methods began to approach me with the hope of learning my secrets. Some of them were ascetics without the burden of family life, who had practised meditation for years in seclusion. I was baffled. Why should such persons approach me? Why should this role be thrust upon me? I am a government officer and was content to be so. I did not have the training, knowledge, capacity or inclination to be a spiritual path-finder for others. Yet, here I was in a role I had least expected to play. Mystical are the ways of the Divine.

I wanted to find out if similar things had been happening to others. Many people came to me with experiences which had been both wondrous and touching. Some of them had definitely been miraculous. Sai Baba's life had been full of miracles. One almost every day, every hour and every moment. These miracles continue to take place even today. There could be no better example than that of Anil, a young business-man of Delhi. He had been an ardent devotee of Shri Sainath for the last 15 years. In 1984, his one-year-old son was found to have a serious medical problem and had to be taken to London for treatment. The child suffered from Down's Syndrome with chromosomic deficiency, a combination usually very fatal. The doctors advised surgery, though they were not fully hopeful of a cure. Anil had unimpeachable faith in Sainath, who had said "Why worry when I am there?" The child unfortunately expired on the operation table. Anil had been sure all along that the child would recover from the operation, so much so that he had even organised a birthday party for him on the fourth day from the day of operation.

The death of the child was doubly shocking to Anil. His only child had passed away. Worse still, his God had failed him. Before consigning the mortal remains of the child to flames, Anil took the pendant of Shri Sai from his neck and put it around the child's neck, praying that he should be given back to him. Clearly, despite the severe loss and despite a sense of having been cheated, faith had not deserted him as yet.

Miraculously, Anil's wife conceived the same month. Wiser with the death of the child, the couple underwent an embryonic Down's Syndrome test. The first test was positive. The couple prayed continuously to Baba for His divine intervention. Once again everything seemed lost. They prayed to Baba fervently. The second test two days later indicated that the child was free from all chromosomic deficiencies. A healthy son was born to Anil in the ninth month. To everyone's utter surprise, the newborn bore a mark of the size and same colour (blue) on his hip-line like the earlier child had. Anil had, in his faith, already announced that Baba would definitely give back his son. His faith in Sai is truly a matter of emulation.

There have been several instances like this, too innumerable to mention, during the existence of Baba in gross form and thereafter. There have been cases of several Anils which have not come to light, or which cannot be recounted for want of space. The fact remains that Sai is there for all who care to seek Him. Those who seek with humility and with a pure heart, Sai never fails them. Those who have sought once, have found Sai for ever. I continue to receive letters in scores every day, narrating more and more of such instances. I wonder within myself, from where does He get the time to attend to the millions of problems of seekers?

Sai's Life — A Divine Mystery

The early life of Sai Baba, till his appearance at Shirdi, has been shrouded in mystery. There have been a number of theories regarding his birth, the identity of his parents, his birth place, his childhood, his education, the miracles he must have performed during this period, his spiritual training, etc. We have no means to verify the authenticity, in absence of which, they remain at their best, only apocryphal, and speculative in character, based upon unfounded testimony. These speculations, further, are also mutually contradictory. Some of them even contradict themselves. This renders them even more dubious.

As for the Baba, he discouraged all questions relating to his parentage, his early life and his background. It once so happened that a thief was arrested by the police and stolen property recovered from his person. In order to save himself the thief stated that he had received the stolen property from Baba. The fame of Baba had already reached far and wide. He had numerous followers and *Bhaktas*. It was a charge to which few would give any credence. Yet, in order to clear the name of Baba, the Dhulia Court appointed a Pleader Commissioner to examine Baba and to record his statement. The situation was ridiculous, as it would appear. The 'Spirit Incarnate' was being examined by 'matter'. Yet, Baba chose to co-operate with the Commissioner. This situation had arisen about six centuries earlier in the days of Hazrat Nizamuddin

Auliya, one of the greatest Sufi Saints of this land. He was faced with charges levelled by overtly jealous members of the *Ulema*. The Hazrat was summoned by the Sultan to appear and to answer the charges. It was not necessary for the Hazrat to appear. Endowed, as he was, with vast supernatural powers, there was little within the capacity of the Sultan to compel his attendance. The Hazrat was a force within himself, which no material force could subdue. Yet, he chose to appear. He did not want to miss an opportunity to educate the *Ulema*, whose bigoted nature was well known. He, further, did not want to weaken the temporal authority of the Sultan. His refusal to appear would have surely marked an end to the Sultan's Rule. Sri Sai Baba also consented to subject himself to an examination by the Commissioner appointed by the Court. On being questioned by the Commissioner on his parentage he replied that 'Brahma' (the Supreme Being) was his father and 'Maya' (Prakriti) his mother. He had been born out of their union. It is this union of the Brahma with Maya that has been responsible for the creation of this universe. It is a part of the creative process. It is ever-constant and continuous. The Sai had, thus, symbolically indicated his oneness with the Supreme Being. It may also mean that the Sai had never been born, like the others have been. He was truly an '*Ajanma*' i.e. without birth. He acquired that human form for a purpose. Even his *Mahasamadhi* was an act of illusion. He never passed away. There may be no remains inside his Samadhi, who knows. In the past, the rival groups of Muslims and Hindus wanted to take possession of the mortal body of Kabir, to carry out last rites according to their own religious rites. When they took off the cloth from the body of Kabir, they found flowers. They divided the flowers and carried on the rituals. The Sai is as alive today as he ever was. It was, of course, fully established by corroborative evidence of the 'village diary' that the thief had been falsely implicating Baba. In fact, Baba was always equivocal when faced with such questions. He would either be evasive or highly mystical in his replies.

Here, I have collected together some of the popular theories regarding the origin of the Baba. I must confess that the work is rather eclectic in character. There has been no analysis on my part, though at places I have given my own interpretation of some of the events narrated. I have merely stated the theories as they have been propounded in a chronological manner.

This has been purposely done. Some of the prevalent theories have been detailed as here under:

(i) Mhalsapathy has been one of the closest devotees of Baba. He used to serve Baba with utmost devotion and slept with Baba at night in the mosque, which Baba had fondly christened Dwarkamayee. Baba had confided to Mhalsapathy one night, that his parents had been Brahmins belonging to a village named Pathri. His family had a spiritual, religious background. Baba had been handed over to a fakir in his early childhood. Mhalsapathy had observed that some devotees from Pathri would visit Baba regularly and Baba would make enquiries from them about the residents belonging to that place.

It is speculated that the Fakir in question was a Sufi and the Guru of Baba, with whom he had spent many years of his early life. The Baba had great devotion for his Guru and would always speak of him in apotheosistic terms. The devotion of Baba for his Guru is well-known otherwise also, and has been the subject of so many folk songs and folk tales.

(ii) In another book, it has been mentioned that Shri Sainath had been born at Pathri, a village on the banks of the river Godawari. His parents had been highly religious, but issueless. Lord Shiva had blessed them that they would have a son, as a consequence of which, Sri Sainath had been born. The parents however, on account of their detachment from the affairs of the world, had consigned the child to the care of God. A fakir and his wife, who had been passing by, had found the child, accidentally, under a tree in the jungle where he had been abandoned by his parents. The issueless couple were delighted. They brought the child up as their own. The child showed no inclinations whatsoever to take up the chores of this world in his teenage. He was always found deep in the worship of Lord Shiva. Disgusted, the fakir drove him out of his house. The child Sai wandered about in a state of mendicancy till he came to Shirdi where he stayed rooted for the rest of his life.

(iii) Das Ganu Maharaj was a close disciple of Baba. As a police officer, he went to Shirdi to test the veracity of Baba as a God-realised soul. There, in the process he stood fully exposed himself. He was claimed forever by Baba and became one of His principal devotees. His bottled-up devotion for Baba found outlet in the panegyrics and songs that he wrote about His Glory, and these have since become household songs in Maharashtra. Das Ganu was to Baba what Bhai Mardana was to Guru Nanak. He has given some details of Baba's early life in his book *Bhakti Saramrita* (Chapter 26).

One Keshav Rao, a resident of village Jamb Avar in Maharashtra, had been a staunch devotee of Lord Venkatesh (Lord Vishnu). As he was childless, he prayed to Him for a son. Lord Vishnu appeared to him in a dream and intimated that Swami Ramanand of Kashi would be born to him as a son in order to complete the cycle of his karma. In due course, a son was born to Keshav Rao. The child exhibited signs of intense spiritualism and renunciation from the beginning. His father had him married off in order to provide wordly allurements to him. However, the child showed least interest in worldly affairs. He would provide the poor and the needy with alms, food and clothing within his limited resources. Not satisfied with these limited acts of charity, he left his home and settled at a place called Salure (Selawadi) in Maharashtra. There he gradually rose to become the *Jagirdar* in the Nizam's Estate by dint of his labour and on account of his excellent qualities, and was popularly known as Zamedar Gopal Rao. Unlike other *Jagirdars* of his tribe, Gopal Rao spent his resources in fulfilling the needs of the poor and distressed. Gradually miraculous powers manifested themselves in him. He restored the sight of a blind lady by application of chilli powder — a cure by counter elements, and healed many other people by most unconventional methods.

Zamedar Gopal Rao during his lifetime undertook pilgrimages to various places including Kashi. When he went to pay his obeisance at the Durgah of the Sufi saint Suwag Shah at Ahmednagar, a stentorian voice called out to him from within the Durgah, "Ten miles from the town of Manmath your disciple Kabir will be the child of a fakir." The voice also told Gopal Rao that he (Gopal Rao) had been Ramanand, the Guru of Kabir in his last birth. The fakir had desired at his death-bed that Zamedar Gopal Rao would look after the child. Soon thereafter, the widow of a fakir came to see him with a five-year-old child. Gopal Rao accepted the child and brought him up. When he was twelve years old, his mother expired, leaving him all alone with his Master.

The companionship between the child and Gopal Rao, also known as Gopal Rao Maharaj, was constant and divine. Once Gopal Rao went to a dense forest with the child and di not return for about four months. The jealous relatives of Gopal Rao held the child responsible for his disappearance.

They thought the boy's mother had cast a spell on him and after her demise, her son now held Gopal Rao captive in his spell. Consumed with hatred, they searched for Gopal Rao and the child in the forest with revenge in their hearts. When they found the two sitting at a place they started stoning the boy. One of the bricks hurled at the boy hit Gopal Rao on his head. Gopal Rao started bleeding and the wound had to be treated by tying a piece of cloth. According to a different version, the brick did not hit the Guru, but remained hanging in mid-air at his command. The child was so unhappy at the plight of his Guru, that he begged Gopal Rao to send him away, lest further damage be done by the irate relatives of Gopal Rao.

Gopal Rao replied: "I have but a little time to spend on this earth. Today, I shall give you everything that I have and go to Selu." He directed the child to fetch milk from a black cow. Such a cow was found, but it would not give any milk as it was not lactating. The Master touched the udders of the cow. Miraculously, milk started to flow in full view of all those who stood watching. The Master then directed the disciple to take three seers, saying "The three seers of milk given to you represent *Karma*, *Bhakti* and *Gyana*."

Having taken the milk, the disciple at once felt the cosmic transformation within himself. In whatever direction he looked, he saw the omniscience of *Narayana*. The image expanded till the entire universe was filled with *Narayana*. It was then that the Master reminded him "Remember that thou art Kabir, reborn. You were a *grihastha* (householder) in your previous incarnation; you shall remain a celibate in this life. You had used *kirtan* (devotional chorus chanting) as your tool. Now you shall practise *mauna* (silence). Remain at one place and raise those who surrender themselves unto you." The Master further revealed: "My work on this earth is now over.

I shall proceed to Selu where I shall enter my *Mahasamadhi*." Saying this, the Guru then removed the bandaged cloth from his own head and tied it around the head of his disciple. The disciple kept that brick and that cloth throughout his life as a memory of his Guru.

The person whose brick had injured the Master fell dead suddenly. The pursuers then realised their mistake and, falling at the feet of the Master, they prayed that the dead person be forgiven his misdeeds and brought back to life. The Master said that He had transferred all his powers to the boy. Thereupon they requested the boy to bring back the person to life. The Master directed young Sai to restore the person. The disciple took some dust from under the feet of the Master and applied it to the forehead of the dead body. Lo and behold, the dead person immediately stirred back to life and opened his eyes. He fell at the feet of the Master and begged forgiveness. The crowd was astounded. Raising a dead person to life is a miracle which the people fail to comprehend. No doubt, it is a miracle of the highest order, for it involves rising above the law of nature and controlling it The assemblage hailed the Master and his disciple and took them in a procession to Selu. The following day, the Master entered *Mahasamadhi*. The disciple put on the *kafni* and travelled along the southern bank of the Godavari till he finally settled down at Shirdi. This boy was none other than Shri Sainath Himself.

(iv) Shivamma Tayee, the 103-year-old devotee of Shri Sainath used to live in Bangalore before her demise a few years ago. For about fifteen years, till the *Mahasamadhi* of Shri Sainath, she had been staying at Shirdi intermittently and rendering personal services to Baba. In the ninth chapter of the book *My life with Sri Shirdi Sai Baba* titled "What I know about the birth and early life of Shirdi Sai Baba", she mentions Shri Sai's childhood.

Shri Sainath was the child of a Brahmin couple named
Vithala and Chakrapani Amma. Before the birth of Shri Sai,
many children born to this couple had died. When Sainath
was in His mother's womb, she suddenly started getting labour
pains when the couple were walking through a forest
belonging to the territory of the Nizam of Hyderabad. The
husband searched for a place and found a cow shed where the
child was born. Immediately after birth a Fakir came and told
the father, "This boy is not an ordinary person. He is going to
be a universal Master for all living beings. He is nothing but
God's incarnation. I shall come after three months to the same
place in this forest and take this child with me." After three
months the Fakir appeared and prevailed upon the unhappy
parents to give away the child named Babu. The Fakir and
his wife reared the child. When the child was five years old,
the Fakir requested his wife to hand over the child to
Venkusha, a devotee of Balaji living in Selu village. In the
meantime God appeared in a dream to Venkush and told him
"I am coming to you in a dream to Venkusha and told him "I
am coming to you in the form of a boy to become your disciple.
In his previous birth that boy was Kabir Das." The next day,
the fakir's wife brought the boy along with her to Venkusha.

"The very next day the child Baba came with the fakir to
Guru Venkusha." As soon as he (Venkusha) saw the boy
(Baba), his entire body was frozen like ice. No action or
movement could be experienced by him. He called Him
(Baba) thrice as, "Kabir Das, Kabir Das, Kabir Das" and then
he became all right.

Among all his disciples, Venkusha loved Baba the most,
which caused jealousy among the other disciples. One day,
when Venkusha was in penance and Baba was sitting before
him, one of the jealous disciples threw a brick at Baba. Baba
raised His hand immediately and the brick was suspended in

mid-air. Venkusha came back to normal consciousness and told Baba to call the brick. Baba did so and the brick came to His hands. Venkusha told Baba "When the brick breaks, the time will come for you to attain *Samadhi*." The Guru asked Baba to fetch some cow's milk. The Guru then blessed Him saying, "You should spread this message to all human beings that we should not have any disparities (differences). We should respect each other and treat everyone with love, affection, gentleness and kindness. I bless you that those who prostrate before your photo or statue would not suffer the shortage of anything."

Just then the boy who had thrown the brick at Baba fell dead. Soon the jealous people realised their mistake and requested Shri Venkusha to save the boy. At the behest of the Guru, Baba (Shri Sainath) called the dead boy by name and surprisingly, the boy came back to life.

(v) There is another linked version. Shri Sainath always carried a brick with Him. He used it as a pillow while sleeping. Baba told Nanasaheb Chandorkar: "This brick is my Guru's gift to me. It is the object of my meditation. When it breaks, my body must die." Baba further told Chandorkar: "When I was with my Guru in a forest in the district of Parbani (Nizam's state) near Selu, some wicked men hurled bricks and stones at me with murderous intent. One of the bricks, though aimed at me, struck my Guru's head. This is that brick. My Guru's powers were wondrous. This brick remained suspended in mid-air for one and half hours and it would have remained so indefinitely. Its force, however had to be terminated by hitting somebody. My Guru, therefore, offered his own head and in the process saved me. See Nana, how lofty are the souls of the saints."

Just prior to his *Mahasamadhi*, the brick accidentally slipped out of the hands of the boy sweeping the floors of

Dwarkamayee Masjid and broke into two pieces. On seeing this, Baba cried out: "This brick is now broken; the fate of my body has been sealed. It is now time to cast off this body." A short time later He entered His *Mahasamadhi*.

(vi) Shri Sai Sharnanand Swami has given an account of the disclosures made by the Baba regarding His early life in a book entitled *Shri Sai The Superman* (Chapter II). According to this account, Shri Sainath left His parents and came to the banks of the Ganges; the Baba always referred to Godavari as the Ganges. He shifted to Shirdi where He found his Master. The name of His Master was Shah Roshan Mian. Baba served His Master with unflinching devotion for 12 years. Pleased with His services the Master blessed Him: "Wherever you are, here or beyond the seven seas, I will ever be with you to guard and protect you." The *Guru* demanded only two forms of fee (*Dakshina*) from his disciples - *Nishta* (absolute faith) and *Saburi* (patience). These two virtues constitute the essence of the Sai path.

I have deliberately avoided giving another theory of my own, regarding the origin and the early life of Baba. It is a mystery, which no one knows with certainty. It is divine because the Sai is divine. However, there are spiritually advanced souls even today, who are in constant communion with Shri Sai. It is not a mystery for them, though it is certainly divine. The all-embracing Baba knew that the human civilisation was divided between those worshipping the form of God (*Sakara*) and those worshipping God without form (*Nirakara*). He, therefore, permitted His worship in both forms. Not only did His devotees see Him in the form of their own deities like Shri Rama, Shri Krishna, etc. but also in the form of their *Gurus* when He was at Shirdi.

Further, even today, devotees are seeing Him in gross physical form decades after his *Mahasamadhi*. His body was a purposeful creation of God for the people who otherwise could not have been drawn to Him on a purely mental plane. It is not necessary for such a Divine spirit to be born of parents (*Yaunik* creation). He might have been born without parents (*Ayonik*), who knows! Even Christ was born of a Virgin. The spirit of Shri Sai yet remains in the same form. All that the devotees have to do is to follow the path he had indicated, each within his own religion.

'Love' has been the symbol of Sai. This 'love' of Sai is cosmic love, embracing all species and creation. It has no confines, no limitations, no restrictions, no inhibitions, no waxing and waning. It is synonymous with cosmic consciousness.' His life was a lesson in simplicity and utmost sacrifice, which no ordinary man can ever achieve. This was the Baba, whose origin we try to seek. 'Divinity' has no beginning, nor an end. What purpose then, would a debate on it serve? Why waste time on fruitless intellectualism as to how Christ had been born of Virgin Mary, rather than concentrating on how He suffered to alleviate the suffering of mankind? Is it not enough that He was the Messiah who ameliorated the lives of countless millions of humanity and of those to follow? Is not Sai doing the same thing even today? If, as Sai said, He had no beginning and no end and was always there as a part of creation, it would lad to the question "What was there before Creation?" The answer is: Space and the Ancient One (*Ananta Purusha*). *Ananta Purusha* is the Divine soul in 'time eternal'. Many universes come and go at His Will. He is the basis of the Creation continuum. The Sai is the Space and that *Adi Purusha*. How can we seek His origins? Even the *Vedas* are silent on this. So why should we speculate fruitlessly?

The Divine Journey of the Soul

T he creation, its beginning; the Creator, His motives and objectives behind creation; the soul, its attributes; the stages of evolution of creation, etc. have been the subject matter of intense metaphysical inquiry and speculation. Each of the established religions, with perhaps the lone exception of Buddhism, has had its own theories regarding these aspects of creation. Within the parameters of these religions, different schools have propagated their own theories. Even the later Buddhism addressed itself to the task of defining the supernatural and the journey of the soul before birth and after death. All these theories make the situation appear highly complicated to a lay seeker. In the Middle Ages, and even after, these theories had laid the foundations of religious conflicts and wars. Even to the present day, disputes regarding divinity continue to fashion the relations between different societies, often giving rise to communal violence in the process. The task in the present chapter is not to add yet another theory to the existing library of theories. It is, in fact, to reconcile the conflicting theories propounded in different ages and to present a harmonised version of these theories. It is only the 'revealed' and the 'divine' and also the 'God-realised' who can throw light on such matters. Shri Sai, during his lifetime, did not lay much emphasis on 'life after death'. What mattered most to Him was how people prepared for it. In fact, He was never in favour of propounding complex theories. It was not because He was unaware: it is a recorded fact that the learned pandits, consulted Him on most complex matters of the *Shastras*, to their utmost satisfaction. It was simply because Shri Sai was moved by the plight of the suffering humanity in pre-independent India and made it His mission to bring about a qualitative revolution in their lifestyle. It was by no means a sudden outbreak, but rather a gradual and silent revolution, to which all of us continue to be witnesses. Shri Sai, in the course of His discussions, has revealed enough on metaphysics, to fill several volumes. It is simply that these have not been recorded in a systematic manner.

There are five theories prevalent about the beginning of creation and the Divine Manifestation. All religions, all scriptures and all saints of all religions are agreed upon one thing: there was a time when nothing was there. There was no manifestation of the Divine. This state of 'nothingness' or 'absolute void' prevailed before the beginning of the manifestation. Even the concept of 'space' was not there. All saints, incarnations, gods and goddesses, deities and spirits were not there. Only God or *Ananta* existed in a non-manifest manner. The age of this stage of non-manifestation is beyond determination in our conventional yardstick of years and light years.

It was at this time, that He manifested Himself in the most primordial of all forms. As to why God thought of manifesting Himself, is speculated by scriptures of different religions and 'spiritually' evolved persons. The concept of Hinduism in this regard is that of *Sankalp* (Divine Will). According to some, God wanted to see His own image in multi-dimensional forms. According to some others, the *Param Brahma* (the Supreme Being) wanted to play the Divine Game (*Leela*), for fulfilment of His Happiness and, therefore,

He manifested Himself. However, as to why He manifested Himself, even the *Vedas* have remained silent. Using the word *Iti* which would approximately mean the 'final culmination' or 'that beyond which is not', the *Vedas* have preferred not to extend themselves beyond this stage. This stage could also be described as the 'Beyond the Beyond' stage of God. Other religions call it 'The Dark Mist', which during the course of their spiritual journey, no saints have ever reached. The Beyond stage is that of 'Trinity'. How did the God from the Beyond stage come to 'Beyond the Beyond' stage? This remains, as stated, a divine mystery, which has defied all satisfactory explanations by scriptures of all religions, including the *Vedas*.

The moment the Supreme Being had the slightest Divine Will of 'manifestation' in Him, there was a little movement, of the subtlest nature. This produced a ripple. This ripple signified the beginning of creation. That Will of God which created the ripple is also known as *Shakti*. Shakti is the creative energy within the Supreme Being, an outward reflection of His Will. It is the source of all creativity. When this Divine Creativity is withdrawn, the ripples also subside. The energy creating the ripple is withdrawn unto Him. At this stage, God reverts to the original state. This means an end to all creations, all activities, all manifestations, all forms, all matter and all that we can think of. Therefore, the *Kriyasheel Brahma* or the Manifested Supreme Being is the *Prakriti* (Creation). It is the action of the *Kriyan* (Divine Will) with the *Prakriti*, while 'Creation devoid of Will to Manifest' is the *Brahma* (the Supreme Being). Anything perceivable through the sense perception of a man or the supramental consciousness of a saint, is within the parameters of this phenomenon of the ripple. The different universes coming and going, the distant stars, the galaxies and milky ways are all parts of the *Prakriti*, which has been given rise to by this Manifestation. The Hindu

Trinity of *Brahma*, *Vishnu* and *Mahesh*, the pantheon of gods, all constitute a part of the *Prakriti*.

The first ripple of the Divine Will, according to the *Vedas*, created what is known as the *Hiranyagarbha*. The word *hiranya* in Sanskrit means gold. In other words, it is an effulgent intense energy field shining like millions of bulbs, emitting brilliant golden light. *Hiranya* also means, therefore, the light or *jyoti* which was not only shining but was also radioactive. It had radioactive substances within it, from which the elements came out to blend with the cosmic egg. The subject of *Hiranyagarbha* is so extensive that it is possible to write not one chapter, but an entire book on it. However, given the limitations of the present work, it is not possible to write about the periodicity of the manifestation of the 'cosmic field' or the *Hiranyagarbha*. The *Vedas* say that the *Hiranyagarbha* consists of the *Panchbhoot* or the five basic elements of nature — sky, water, light, *vyom* or space and matter or earth. According to Science, the 'cosmic egg' emits a high-density cloud consisting of neutrons and proton particles (Hawking and Carl Sagan). This condensed egg, because of the extreme inner temperature, had a release point with the material pushing from the centre outwards in a siphon action. It is apt to mention here that the first ripple created by the Divine Will is the basis that created the *Hiranyagarbha* and through the *Hiranyagarbha*, the materials of creation. These are what are known as the *Ishwar Tatwa* or the *Nad Brahma* (the Cosmic Sound). Shakespeare called it the 'music of the spheres'. What Moses saw was the 'sonorous light' or the light that spoke. It was the light that gave sound which ordered the Ten Commandments.

The *Hiranyagarbha*, because of the extreme temperature in the core, siphoned out the inner material with a terrible bang (Big Bang). This bang took place on the outer surface of the *Hiranyagarbha*, as the energy rushed out. It was said to be in the form of a disc, according to Western science. It had sharp pointed edges, like the petals of a lotus flower, as per Hindu mythology. This was actually *Brahma*. *Vishnu* was created out of the *Anantagarbha* or the core of the *Hiranyagarbha*. He is represented by a figure asleep upon the bed of *Seshnag* with a lotus growing out of His navel, upon which *Brahma* is seated. The stem of the lotus symbolises the process of siphoning of the energy. That is why the *Vishnu Puran* depicts *Brahma* as coming out of the navel of *Vishnu*. The navel represents the passage to the core. It is an outward manifestation or a symbolic representation of the Big Bang.

The bang had lasted for scarcely 1/10 million of a second. The extended energy filled up the entire space. It was so powerful that the primordial energy rushed out to occupy the vacant region in an un-imaginable speed. The Hindus call it the *Tej Megh* (or the luminous clouds). The velocity of the mighty force created at that time continues even today(the Expanding Theory of the Universe). Science today talks in terms of the Receding Universe or the Receding Nebulae. Parts of the universe continued to shift through what is known through the 'red shift'. Thus, high-density energy clouds spread all over and at a certain point they started creating nebulae. Gradually, these nebulae began to snowball and gained in energy and compactness. They came to be known as stars. In *Rudra Puran*, the stars are known as *Rudras* (*Rudratiti Rudra* or that which is burning). The stars differ in their size and density. Usually, they remain in a constellation, balancing each other by their gravitational force. It is the energy field that keeps the constellation of stars grouped together. This is known in Hindu mythology as the *Ganapati* (Gana means a group and pati means the leader). All constellations and stars cover the space and together they are as the cosmos or Brahmanda.

The sun, a medium star, was formed 630 crore years ago. According to Science, it has lived through half of its life. It is from the sun that the earth emanated by the same process as the blast of the sun at an extreme temperature of 6000 million degrees Celsius. From 'Beyond the Beyond stage' to the formation of the sun only one factor changed to another factor and so on. The Divine Will changed to Divine Consciousness(*Ishwar Chetana*). It manifested itself in perceptible energy fields. These energy fields of the sun or for that matter, of the entire constellation of stars was created out of the consciousness. Therefore, whatever be the manifestation of energy, it continues as a form of Divine onsciousness.

When the earth came out of the sun, a third change occurred. The Divine Consciousness changed to energy and then to gross elements like water, earth, stone, etc. This was the grossest level of God's manifestation and was the end of the downward travel of the Supreme Consciousness. From this point onward, the consciousness started its homeward journey. When the miniscule organic life-form was created, it was an improvement upon the earlier grosser consciousness of stones and metals. An organic substance basically has auto growth, automation and autoproliferation. The earlier grosser elements like stones and metals did not have this. The manifestation of God thereafter began appearing in the form of cosmic consciousness gradually, first in the form of fish, then amphibians, birds, animals, etc. Before the birth of man, the animals had greater consciousness than all other species. In man God found His own image, though only to a limited extent. The Divine Consciousness has blossomed to its maximum or the highest Creative Self in man. There are additional factors to distinguish him from the earlier species. Firstly, man has been given the consciousness that God exists.

Secondly he has been given a part of God's power to control nature by his own initiative. For example, the dinosaurs and other such species could not control nature. They survived as long as they could adjust with nature. However, the moment the two fell into disharmony and the creatures failed to adjust to the changed requirements of nature, they perished.

Man has been the image of God because he has superior power over other species. He can create electricity out of water and even nuclear energy etc. He can control temperature, travel into space, transplant human organs, etc. This is the part of the Divine Power, which has been given over to man. However man, being the latest stage of evolution of the Divine or Cosmic Consciousness has exhibited two trends. The first of these is the display of the consciousness of being a part of the Divine Will which created it. The second trend is the exhibition of the gross consciousness of various levels of life foms on this earth, the animals, birds and other living beings. The homeward journey of the Divine Consciousness would mean greater realisation of the original stage and abandoning the grosser impressions which he has gathered during the process of evolution in an increasing manner. It is actually man who shortened the process of evolution; not all, but some men have the capacity of shortening it at will. Men can rise to heights Divinity; several of them have. Apart from the powers obtained through the use of modern of Science, saints have exhibited much greater control over nature than scientists can ever dream of. The miracles of Shri Sai and those performed by other saints exhibit a complete command over the elements of nature. Raising a person from the dead, healing by touch, bringing rains, sunshine, etc. reflects the powers of their command. No one has heard of a monkey or an elephant exercising these powers. When these powers are used in accordance with the Divine law, they are highly creative.

The World of Shri Sai –
Yesterday, Today & Tomorrow

Shri Sai Baba of Shirdi lived in Shirdi, a small village in the state of Maharashtra in India, for about sixty years between 1858 and 1918. Earlier He was at and around Shirdi for about two years between 1852 and 1854. When He first arrived He was in a God-intoxicated state, without any consciousness of His own body, of society or of time. He used to sit and meditate under a neem (margosa) tree, wander around and live all by Himself. A kind village woman called Bayaji took pity on Him and used to search Him out and force Him to eat. One day in 1854, He suddenly disappeared, only to reappear in 1858. No one knows where He was and what He did during this period.

The exact date and place of birth, family name and parentage of Baba are still shrouded in mystery, although researchers speculate that He was born in a village called Pathri now in Maharashtra (India), somewhere between 1835 and 1838. Whether He was a Hindu or a Muslim is still not clear, because Baba never encouraged questions on such issues. He sported a beard and moustache, donned a long robe and head gear like some of the Sufis, and yet had a perforation in the ears like the Hindus. He spoke in Urdu, Hindi, Maharashtrian and some South Indian languages. He participated in Hindu and Muslim festivals. His approach in short, was universal and humanitarian.

On His second arrival, He stayed in a dilapidated mosque on the outskirts of Shirdi for about sixty years, although He spent some nights in an adjacent place called Chawdi. He used to be visited by some fakirs and Sufis and also Hindu sadhus. He used to beg in a few houses daily in Shirdi and share His food with dogs, birds and poor people. For some time He used to treat people by administering some kind of herbal medicine. Initially, the local Hindu community looked upon Him with suspicion, but when they found the kind fakir was able to help them through miraculous methods, people like Tatya Kote Patil the farmer, Mhalsapathy the goldsmith, Shyama the school teacher, Das Ganu the police officer Nanasahed Chandorkar the magistrate, Buti the rich money lender from Nagpur, Kakasaheb Dixit the solicitor from Bombay, Abdul and hundreds of others from different places flocked around him. All of them and their families got direction and solace, as well as material and spiritual support from Baba. His name spread gradually to many parts of India and hundreds of visitors started coming to Shirdi every day, as if visiting a temple. Their experiences with Sai spread His name further and became the folk lore of that time. Worship of Shri Sai and the composition of devotional songs about him started then. The mosque known as Dwarkamayee looked like the court of a king, with thousands of people appearing before Baba for help and the *Sadguru* helping them every day.

Shri Sai renovated the mosque and the temples in Shirdi and got the village well cleaned. Baba planted trees with His own hands on a piece of land which is now known as the Lendibagh garden. He created an atmosphere of mutual support covering all aspects of social life in the villages. He participated in all religious festivals, encouraged group dining and group worship to bring all the devotees together. He got built three rest houses called *wadas* with the help of His devotees. These rest houses, called Sathewada, Butiwada and Dixitwada were built for the convenience of the visiting devotees. At times Shri Sai even used to cook food Himself and serve the devotees, and cured their sickness by giving the sacred ash from His fireplace called the *Udi*. This practice continues even today and the people are getting the benefit. He even took care of the animals and birds in the village. He was the biggest social reformer of His time, because of which many of His devotees started similar humanitarian activities wherever they went. Nationalist leaders like Bal Gangadhar Tilak and others used to visit Him for solace and direction.

Shri Sai left His bodily form on 15th October 1918. His body was entombed in a place called "Samadhi Mandir". The Samadhi Mandir, Dwarkamayee Mosque, Chawdi, Lendibagh, the Gurusthan with the sweet neem tree, and the temples of Khandoba, Hanuman, Ganesh and Shani are the places visited by devotees.

During his lifetime Shri Sai never set up any institution or place of worship in His name. After His departure, Shri Shirdi Sai Baba Trust of Shirdi came into existence and also a magazine called "Sai Leela", which is being published regularly. These are the works of the devotees. Today in India, there are a few thousand temples of Baba and hundreds of trusts have been formed. A large number of books written by Indian and foreign authors, hundreds of magazines/journals and reading material in almost all Indian languages have been published.

The trust, on behalf of the government of Maharashtra, looks after the day-to-day running of the temple. To cope with the ever-increasing number of devotees, a rest house (500 rooms) and all other facilities like hospital, drinking water, restaurants, dining halls, etc. have been constructed. It is a lively place, vibrant with the spirit of Sai. Shirdi is at a distance of about 6 hours from Bombay, 4 hours from Pune, 2 ½ hours from Aurangabad and 1½ hours from Nasik by road, and is well-connected with bus and taxi services. Besides, Bombay, Aurangabad, and Pune have airlinks. The nearest railway point is Kopergaon at a distance of about 75 kms from Shirdi. There are more than fifty hotels in Shirdi of different categories, suitable to the financial capacity of the devotees. In fact, the entire social, economic and religious life of Shirdi centres around Shri Sai's tomb.

There are only two or three persons still alive who had seen Shri Sai in their childhood, to tell posterity what a God on earth looked like, and how compassionate He was to all of them. Most of the books written on Baba, vividly describe the devotees' experiences. During Baba's time, and even today, devotees are experiencing Baba's kindness and help in times of need. Baba had promised that even after His departure, His tomb would speak and He would continue to help His devotees whenever He was remembered with faith and love. The most important book written on Baba with His blessings, originally in Marathi verse by Shri Govind Raghunath Dhabolkar alias Hemadpant is called *Shri Sai Satcharitra*. Its translated version in English, Hindi and other Indian languages has been brought out by the Shirdi Sai Sansthan. Every devotee should read the book to have an understanding of Baba's personality and deeds.

There is a routine of four group prayers (*Aartis*) in the early morning (0530 hours), at noon (1200 hours), at sunset (1600 hours) and at night (2130 hours) in front of Baba's tomb and statue. Besides, special *poojas* of Baba and *Satyanarayana poojas* are performed. *Ram Navami* (considered the birthday of Baba), *Guru Poornima* and (*Dussehra*) (the day of Baba's *Mahasamadhi*) are celebrated with a lot of pomp and ceremony. The average crowd on these days is about 4 to

5 lakhs and sometimes even more. Every Thursday a photograph of Baba is carried in a palanquin in a procession with music and light.

The devotees of Baba experience and believe, that Shri Sai calls His children to His *Samadhi* as He had promised, and takes care of them.

Only a visit to Shirdi can tell what Shri Sai is and what He was.

Shri Sai Satcharita — A Divine Experience

These days because of many other commitments, I am unable to read much, but there was a time when I used to read a lot. Till three or four a.m. well past midnight, I used to read lying on the bed. At times my eyes would get tired due to reading continuously, but I could not stop myself in the middle of it. I used to wash my eyes and again start reading. I was deeply involved with reading. I used to read in the bathroom, I used to read while travelling, lying down on the sofa, so much so that while having meals also, I used to be engrossed in reading. Even after all this, I was never satisfied, because I was in search of something which I was not able to find. I read widely on *Puranas, Upanishads, Bhagwat, Gorakh Samhita, Dherand Samhita* and the biographies of many saints. I read the *Bible,* the *Quran* and many other books related to Buddhism and Sikhism, etc. I had many of the books photocopied and kept at home. I had developed a close bond with these books.

All this happened around 1989-90, when I was residing in a government bungalow in Netaji Nagar, one of the colonies of Delhi. Inspite of reading so much I was yet not contented, as if I was searching for something from the innermost recesses of my soul. Perhaps, I was searching for my past and also the reason of my birth. I read about many civilisations like *The Book of Dead*, on the Egyptian pyramids and the *Books of Dead*

by the Tibetans and Lamas. I read all such books available in
Hindi, English, Sanskrit, Bengali and my mother-tongue
Oriya, not once or twice but many times over, yet I was not at
peace. I was certainly in search of something, but I was not
able to know what it was that I was searching for ! I also read
about *Kriya Yoga, Dhyana Yoga, Bhakti Yoga, Hatha Yoga,
Tantra-mantra, Puja-vidhi*, etc. All these activities gave me
temporary satisfaction but complete inner satisfaction was still
lacking. I felt as if I was flowing in the stream of an incoherent
consciousness. And then, one day I suddenly came out of
this mind-dominated jungle of knowledge and reached the
habitat where to I belonged. I started seeing the river, the
stars, my dear ones calling me lovingly from afar. Leaving
behind the fetters of the mind, I entered into a world of
simple, spontaneous existence.

This could happen only when the grace of Shri Sainath
Maharaj came on me. I had not heard of His name till 1989.
It seemed as if Shri Sai came to my life to repay some old
debts of my previous births, or as if the fructification of all
my pious deeds of past lives had suddenly taken place. It
seemed as if the Lord, whom my father and all my forefathers
had been worshipping for thousands of years, had at last cast
His merciful and gracious glance on a boy in their family-
line as a consequence of their accumulated merits. When the
Guru Maharaj came and enthroned himself so spontaneously
in my heart, I had nothing more to do. With utter amazement
I watched like an observer, the changes in my thought process
and feelings. After this blessing of Shri Sainath I got immersed
in listening to the *aartis* of Baba. I was seized by an intense
urge to listen to these all the time. How simple and appealing
are the words of Das Ganu Maharaj:

Raham nazar karo ab more Sai !
Tum bin nahin mujhe ma-baap bhai.
Main andha hun banda tumhara
Mein na jaanu Allah-Ilahi.

Caste your merciful glances at me Oh Sai, for I hold you
as my father, mother and brother. I am a blind follower of you
who cannot preceive of any other God that Thou.

I used to do the *aarti* of Baba twice or thrice a day before
His picture at home. The urge to know more and more about
Baba had been so strong that I had collected all the books I
could lay my hands on at Shirdi and Delhi. In those days, not
many books were written on Shri Sai, unlike today. Only ten
or twelve books written in Hindi and English were available.

In 1989, when I visited Shirdi for the first time, I brought
back the Hindi translation of *Shri Sai Satcharitra* with me.
Somebody told me that this was the book which was written
by a modestly educated person called 'Hemadpant', with the
instruction and blessings of Shri Sainath Himself. When I
read this book for the first time, I could somewhat understand
the life-story of Baba. It gives a graphic and captivating
account of the divine events from His life. As I went on
reading, a beautiful but powerful feeling started stirring within
me — a sort of feeling which I was myself unfamiliar with
before. At times I used to read about the same event again
and again about eight to ten times. I used to ask myself
whether all that was written in the book was possible.

Can a bag of wheat flour from a hand-mill, sprinkled on
the village boundary, check the incidence of cholera in that
village? Is it possible to light a lamp with water? Can any
human being stop fire or rain? It seemed as if all these were
imaginary and baseless stories, like the ones found in the
mythologies of the Hindu religion, or stories written by

sentimental devotees to glorify their own guru out of proportion. But when any of them appeared to be true, I used to feel startled and also feel charged with a strange emotion. I used to think in my heart that if all this is true, then "O Sai, why was I not born earlier to witness your divine *leelas*? How unfortunate am I that seventy-two years after your passing away and after spending forty-two years of my life, I could know about you." At times I used to feel so strong a surge of love that I used to close the doors and lie prostrate for long periods before Baba's photo. I could say nothing, but only cry aloud from my heart —

Namaskar Sashtang Shri Sainath,
Namaskar Sashtang Shri Sainath

My only wish at that moment was to breathe my last, uttering these words. But my analytical mind would then draw me back from this stage of intense love and I would come down again to the mundane realities of earthly existence.

Controlling my mental state, somehow, I continued to read *Shri Sai Satcharitra*. As I reached the forty-second chapter, my heart started pounding. The context was : "Readers, up till now, you have heard the stories of Baba's life. Now hear attentively about Baba's passing away......"

As I read the words "Baba's passing away", I suddenly felt deeply hurt. I had been reading His life story so intensely that by the time I had reached this chapter, Baba had unknowingly entered my life, soul and mind just like a living person. Deep in my heart somewhere I had become a part of His life and Shri Sai had become my dearest father and companion. In such a situation time certainly becomes still, as the sense of time in me was lost while reading 'Shri Sai Satcharitra. The moment my eyes read the words "Baba's passing away", I felt jolted and choked with emotion. I was just not able to control the tears pouring from my eyes. There was a shock and shiver in my entire body. I spontaneously went down and kissed Baba's feet and His photo and pleaded tearfully "Baba please don't do this." I prostrated in front of Him and continued to read with some courage in that intense state of mind. I further read "Baba got a slight attack of fever on 28th September, 1918 A.D. The fever lasted for 2 or 3 days; but afterwards Baba gave up His food, and there by He grew weaker and weaker. On the seventeenth day, i.e. Tuesday, the 15th October, 1918, Baba left His mortal coil at about 2.30 P. M."

(*Shri Sai Satcharitra*, Chapter 42, Page 220)

When I was reading it I felt as if my soul was being shattered into pieces. I was feeling extremely helpless — like an orphan who had suddenly lost his father. It was further mentioned that two years before this, i.e. in 1916, Baba had given an indication of His passing away. Further, I read that before His departure Baba gave away His last property of nine rupees in charity to a lady called Laxmibai. Knowing that His devotees might go without food after His departure, He had instructed all the devotees to go and have their food. This pure and unfathomable compassion of Baba for His devotees touched my heart to the core. In those moments of intense agony I was mentally bidding him farewell —

Namaskar Sashtang Shri Sainath,
Namaskar Sashtang Shri Sainath

I was telling Him in my heart - "O Sainath, O ocean of love! I am dazed to see your compassion. If in a thousand lives I am able to be just a dust particle under your feet, then my soul will get peace and life will be meaningful."

Shri Sai Satcharitra further recounts - "The news of Baba's passing away spread like a wild fire in the village of Shirdi and all people, men, women and children ran to the Masjid;

and began to mourn this loss in various ways. Some cried out loudly, some wallowed on in the streets and some fell down senseless. Tears ran down from the eyes of all, and every one was smitten with sorrow. Who could come and console them, when they had lost the God - manifested from amongst them? Who can describe their sorrow?"

(*Shri Sai Satcharitra*, Chapter 43-44, Page 261)

While reading this graphic account, uncontrollable streams of tears kept flowing from my eyes, just as the people of Shirdi must have cried then. I felt as if I had died with Baba at that moment and was awakened before the mortal body of Baba in Shirdi seventy-two years ago. I was observing the body of Baba reclined on the shoulder of Bayaji. With tears I was observing the death of my ideals and my God. With much pain and anguish, I continued reading.

"His passing away is just a worldly formality. He is present in all matter, living or non-living, and He is the sole bearer and the controller of the inner souls of all the beings. This can be experienced even now and many have experienced it, who completely surrendered at His feet and with their whole being worship Him".

(*Shri Sai Satcharitra*, Chapter 43-44, Page 265)

After reading this, my heart was somewhat consoled with the thought that even after leaving His mortal body Baba is still alive, and those whom He had looked after as His children are not without His care today. I remembered the reassuring words of Baba — "I will come running to the help of my devotees even after entering my *Samadhi*," the book said.

Reading this I calmed down and felt some relief from the state of deep agony. Yet the memories about the last moments of Baba would suddenly prick my heart now and then, and I would feel deeply agonised. Even today, when I recollect that scenario I feel extremely sad and helpless.

Shri Sai Satcharitra introduced me to the world of Baba. It took me close to Baba, as a result of which His supreme grace came on me. I developed an inseparable emotional bond with Him. This is also mentioned in *Shri Sai Satcharitra*: "The life stories, parables and teachings of Sai Baba are very wonderful. They will give peace and happiness to the people, who are afflicted with the pain and miseries of this worldly existence, and also bestow knowledge and wisdom, both in the worldly and in spiritual domains. If these teachings of Sai Baba, which are as interesting and instructive as the Ve ic lore, are listened to and meditated upon, the devotees will get what they aspire for viz., union with Brahma, mastery n eight-fold yoga, bliss of meditation, etc."

(*Shri Sai Satcharitra*, Chapter 2, Page 7)

I continued to read *Shri Sai Satcharitra* regularly for about three to four years. In 1993, on the day of *Mahashivratri* I lighted a lamp in front of the photo of Shri Sai Baba sitting on a mat and completed reading, *Shri Sai Satcharitra* within that night. Whenever I went to Shirdi I brought along with me a number of copies of *Shri Sai Satcharitra* in Hindi and English and distributed them among the people.

The evaluation of the greatness of *Shri Sai Satcharitra* in philosophical and spiritual terms brings out some significant facts to us, which will be of great help to those who follow the path of devotion; no matter to which religion, faith or belief, they belong. Those who had spent substantial parts of their lives with Baba like Mhalsapati, Hemadpant, Tatya Kote Patil, Laxmibai Shinde, Das Ganu, Kaka Saheb Dixit, Bapusaheb Jog, Shyama and others, had many direct experiences with Baba. Some intellectual persons like Dada Saheb Khaparde have recorded memories of their Shirdi stay in a diary, and the events described and recorded in it are based on their direct experiences with Baba and established on a factual basis. Neither the characters nor the events mentioned in this book are imaginary. *Shri Sai Satcharitra* is a discourse on the experiences the devotees had with Shri Sai and the preachings of Baba. Baba got it written through Shri Dabholkar by giving inner motivation to him. Baba had clearly told him: "I Myself write my own life. Hearing My stories and teachings will create faith in devotees' hearts and they will easily get self-realisation and bliss...."

(*Shri Sai Satcharitra*, Chapter 2, Page 8)

The significance of *Shri Sai Satcharitra* is :

• This is the first and foremost book based on the life-story of Shri Sai Baba, which was originally composed in Marathi verse form. The writing of the book started in the lifetime of Baba with His blessings.

• The Hindi translation of this book is in simple Hindi language, which can be understood even by a common man.

• The divine truth imparted by this book is even greater than the knowledge contained in the *Vedas* and *Gita*, because all the characters and events in it are real and authentic and have been recorded in detail by many devotees.

• Because of the use of simple Hindi, it is easy for everyone to comprehend it. Today there are very few people who can understand the Sanskrit language properly and absorb the meaning and substance of Sanskrit texts easily.

• The spiritual essence contained in all the religious scriptures like *Vedas*, *Gita* and *Yoga Vashisht* is found in the life-story of Shri Sainath.

• The concepts of God and spirituality are explained in such a simple yet comprehensive manner in *Shri Sai Satcharitra*, that no additional book or commentary is required to understand it. It has a natural flow whereby the readers start feeling as if they had been closely associated with its events in their past lives.

• I may mention here that the glory of Shri Sai is spreading in the world, far and wide, in such an amazing way that detailed information in the websites on Internet about Shri Sai and *Shri Sai Satcharitra* is available for interested readers.

The foremost duty of Sai devotees is therefore to read *Shri Sai Satcharitra* and absorb it into their beings completely. The more they read this book, the more it will bring them closer to Baba and all their doubts and apprehensions will be cleared. It also has been experienced that during a crisis, if any devotee is searching for an answer, if he randomly opens *Shri Sai Satcharitra*, praying to Baba sincerely and with faith, his answer can be found in that open page. Many people have got their desired benefits after reading *Shri Sai Satcharitra* for a week in a *paraayana* form.

Therefore, *Shri Sai Satcharitra* should be utilised by all Sai devotees in the following manner:

(1) Get the book, *Shri Sai Satcharitra* in whatever language one choose to read. Neatly wrap it up in a piece of new cloth, and place it near Baba's photograph or idol with due sanctity.

(2) Whether at home or elsewhere, one should always read a few pages of the book every night before going to sleep. Every devotee should try to keep Baba as the last thought before sleep.

(3) During a crisis it should be read devoutly for a week, as is mentioned in *Shri Sai Satcharitra*. If possible, reading should begin on a Thursday or on some other special day, such as *Ramnavami, Dussehra, Gurupurnima, Janmashtami, Mahashivratri, Navratri*, etc. After its completion on the

seventh day, one should feed the poor and destitute either in the temple or at home or wherever possible.

(4) One should read it sitting in some isolated corner in the temple or in front of Baba's statue or photograph/painting. If other people are present, then it should be read to them or with them as well. Group reading should always be encouraged.

(5) Wherever and whenever possible, it should be read continuously from sunrise to sunset in the temples on auspicious days. Devotees may be asked to read it in turns, as is done in chanting the holy name i.e. *Naamjap*. Encourage children to read this book. Question-answer competitions based on *Shri Sai Satcharitra* can be organised in temples.

(6) *Shri Sai Satcharitra* should be read to the devotees who are sick, aged and those nearing death as much as possible. All of them will get peace.

(7) *Shri Sai Satcharitra* is a reasonably-priced book and is easily available at Shirdi. Therefore, any devotee visiting Shirdi must bring a few copies with him to distribute among the people free of cost.

(8) At times of distress and agony, if one sincerely searches for the answers from *Shri Sai Satcharitra* he will not only find the answers but also solace. His faith will grow in Baba.

I pray to Shri Sainath to reveal the divine knowledge and mysteries contained in this book to the devotees in the same manner in which He had inspired Hemadpant to write this book. *Shri Sai Satcharitra* should be considered by all Sai devotees as the *Gita* and *Bible*.

Shri Sai –The Greatest Assurance

G od has created a manifested material universe around the human soul or *Jiva*. The *Jiva* takes birth from life to life till its *karmas* (both positive and negative) are exhausted. After the *karmas* are exhausted, a human body is not required. Then the soul continues in a body-less state and merges with God, the Over-soul from which it came.

The main function of Shri Sainath, the *Param Sadguru* was to draw out, train, help and evolve the human souls to get rid of their *karmas* and *Jivdasa*. Baba, in an earlier phase of his life must have undergone the various *Jivdasa* Himself. He has narrated many stories about His past lines in *Shri Sai Satcharitra*. Being the Over-soul, He knew about the conditions and the stages of evolution of all souls, and their past. Hence, He could guide and control them effectively. He used to say that He could draw the soul of any of His devotees at the time of death, even from thousands of miles, and also that He knew everything about everyone.

To hold on to such a *Samarth Guru* is the basic as also the ultimate requirement of a real devotee. All prayers, *sadhanas, poojas, yogas* are meant for evolving the soul out of the sufferings and limitations of its human embodiment. Therefore, the *Sadguru* who is capable of taking the human souls to the ultimate reality is the key person. This key person, being beyond life and death himself, is a guide for the many lives of his devotees. Parents are linked with one 'birth' but the *Sadguru* is linked with many births. All human relations, father, mother, wife, children can walk along with a soul till death. But it is the *Sadguru* alone who walks along after death. He is, therefore, our best and permanent friend. We should hold on to him with all the love, devotion and faith we have. One must continue steadfastly with faith, and realise that in this life whatever pleasure and pain we experience are under his guidance and control. These experiences are for the evolution of the soul and are essential. Those who have this faith and patience evolve faster than those who lose patience and faith quickly. Baba said that when faced with a difficult situation, don't break down. Wait and see what happens, because it is my duty to protect my children/devotees at any cost. What better assurance can be given by any one?

Jai Shri Sai

Hazrat Babajan

Hazrat Babajan

Circa 1820	Born in Baluchistan near Quetta. Christened as Gulrukh.
18 years later	Ran away from home to escape marriage.
	Moved to Rawalpindi and maintained ascetic life for some years.
	Spent 17 months in isolation, presumably in a cave.
Circa 1855	Journeyed into Punjab.
Circa 1900	Arrived in Bombay and then after a few months travelled to East & North of India.
April 1903	Made a pilgrimage to Mecca.
1903 – 1907	Reappeared in the Deccan, Poona.
Around 1910	Settled beneath a Neem tree in Char Bavadi Puna. Gained the name Hazrat (the Presence) Baba (Father, since she claimed she was a man) Jan (Soul).
Around 1921	Predicted a fierce storm. The people of Poona constructed a dwelling for her, which connected with the Neem tree.
1921 Sept. 21	Attained Mahasamadhi.

Hazrat Babajan

Today, there stands a humble tomb under a shady neem tree in the cantonment area of Pune, which is visited not only by the common folk of all religions and creeds, but also by spiritual aspirants and saints. The tomb declares the existence of Hazrat Babajan, one of the greatest women Perfect Masters (*Sadgurus*) India ever had. She was so high in the spiritual hierarchy that she used to call even Baba Tazuddin of Nagpur, a spiritual master in the *jeevanmukta* stage (i.e., beyond the cycle of birth and death) and other spiritual masters as her children.

It would be of interest to Sai devotees to know that there was a common link between Hazrat Babajan and Shri Sainath. The devotees of Shirdi Sai Baba are generally aware about his foremost disciple, Upasani Baba Maharaj, who stayed at a place named Sakuri, situated at a distance of about 11 kilometres from Shirdi. One of the main disciples of Upasani Maharaj was Meher Baba, who carried out his spiritual activities from a place known as Meher Nagar in Ahmedabad. At a young age, Meher Baba became a spiritual seeker. In his search for a mentor (*guru*), he travelled far and wide. Ultimately, one day he came to Pune and met Babajan. The latter, who was aware about the spiritual future of Meher Baba, drew him close to her in an affectionate manner and kissed him on the forehead. Meher Baba was at once thrownup to the fourth plane of consciousness and remained in a state of stupor (when spiritual aspirants enter into the fourth plane, that is, when they enter into the world of mental consciousness, they become dazed with the brightness of light they see around). They continue to be in that state of stupor till a competent *guru* brings them down to the normal state of consciousness. In that state, Meher Baba was brought to Shirdi and he prostrated before Sainath. Sainath looked into his eyes deeply, and loudly repeated the word *parvardigar* thrice. Then he sent Meher Baba to Upasani Maharaj, who was staying in the temple. As Meher Baba approached Upasani Maharaj, the latter threw a stone which hit Meher Baba at a point in the middle of the two eyebrows (*bhrukuti*). This instantaneously brought down the consciousness of Meher Baba to the normal plane. Thus Babajan started the work on Meher Baba, which Shri Sainath completed through Upasani Maharaj. Meher Baba stayed for a few years with Shri Upasani Maharaj, before he achieved the state of a Perfect Master himself and moved to Pune.

Babajan, perhaps, had the rare distinction of being the only woman of non-Indian origin who played a significant role in the spiritual life of India, and was unequivocally accepted as a spiritual master. Equally interesting is the crusade of this lonely woman, in a man-dominated society, outside her native soil, to strive and achieve the 'beyond' state of self-realisation. Her exact date of birth is not known. She was possibly born in the year 1820 or a little earlier, to a Pathan chieftain of the Afghans. It seems that she was born in a place on the borders of Baluchistan (now part of Pakistan) near the town Quetta. She was named Gulrukh, (rose-faced), a name aptly given to her by her parents due to her natural beauty. Although born in a rich and aristocratic family, she was contemplative and religious by nature. In her childhood itself, she not only learnt the entire *Quran* by heart, but also went further to interpret it in her own way, much to the surprise of the elders. She did not indulge in the frivolities of life but took to austerity at this young age. Later, when her parents proposed to get her married at the age of fourteen, she would not agree. This was an unusual situation in an orthodox and traditional Pathan society.

It could have been that she was betrothed. However, before her parents could get her married, she left home quietly. According to one version, she fled from home on the wedding day itself. So intense was her spiritual motivation that at the age of eighteen, a beautiful girl like her dared to go out of the *Purdah* system and roam around in the wilderness, risking threats from groups of bandits and warring tribal groups that infested the area. She walked all the way to Peshawar, a passing point between Afghanistan and India. There she linked with the Sufi communities and earned her livelihood doing the work of a servant in a shrine or somewhere else. She then walked about hundred and fifty miles south-east and reached Rawalpindi. There she met the person she was searching for — a Hindu Master, under whose guidance she made rapid spiritual progress. Practising severe austerity in a solitary place in a mountain cave for about seventeen months, she achieved control of both physical and mental desires. Thereafter, she moved from place to place, in the Punjab area, achieving expansion of her consciousness through varied experiences. Ultimately she reached Multan at the age of about thirty-seven. Then she came in contact with a Muslim teacher, who further refined her consciousness within a few months. She again returned to the Hindu teacher at Rawalpindi, who brought down her exalted state of consciousness to the normal state. Unfortunately, the names of both her teachers are not known. Still continuing her spiritual quest, she reached the state of perfection (realisation) at the age of sixty-five. Where she went during these two decades, is not known, but it is certain that she never stayed at one place for long, but moved like a mendicant.

Ultimately, the old matriarch, ripe and ready for her future role, reached Bombay in 1900. At Bombay, she used to stay in the Chunna Bhatti locality near Byculla. She visited Mecca in 1903 and it is likely that she visited Medina. Around 1910 she came to Pune and finally settled under a big neem tree in the Char Bavadi area of the cantonment. Although it was a place where anti-socials and drunkards resided, the Perfect Master decided to make it her 'seat' and stayed there till she left her gross body. No one initially knew who she was, till some Baluchi (native of Baluchistan) soldiers of the British government recognised her. These Baluchi soldiers were surprised and shocked to see this old lady sitting under a neem tree. They remembered that a number of years earlier they had buried her in a grave for calling herself *Anal-Haq* (I am the Truth). The extremist Sunni Ulema had conspired with these soldiers and buried her alive for calling herself 'the ultimate truth' i.e. God. They felt remorseful when they realised that she was no ordinary mortal. They begged her forgiveness and thereafter became her staunchest devotees. During their free time, they sat near her and virtually guarded her at all hours. These soldiers then formed the first group of her 'children', as she affectionately called them.

Soon, people of all religions, Muslims, Zoroastrians and Hindus, started coming to her from far and wide. People started feeling transformed and happy just by looking at her, even though she imparted no formal teachings or theoretical discourses. However, there was something magnetic in her. The feeling of love emanating from her was so strong, that some people started living permanently around the place. There was no limit to her compassion. She would usually give away her clothes and food to the poor people, as she ate very little. Once a thief tried to steal a shawl which she was covered with, while she was sleeping. The thief was able to pull out the whole shawl, except for one portion which was underneath her body. To enable the thief to take the shawl, she raised herself while pretending to be asleep. Similarly, when a thief was caught for having stolen two gold bangles from her wrist by injuring her, she prevented the police from taking any action by not identifying the thief.

Her acts of kindness were numerous, many of which are characteristic of Shirdi Sai Baba. Her blue eyes, her agile body, her distribution of food to the poor, her permanent state of wakefulness (*Sahaja Samadhi*), her stay under the neem tree, her disregard for bodily comforts, are all features common with Shri Sainath. Like Shri Sainath, she also worked through miracles at times, either to help people or to evolve them spiritually. She liked jokes (like all saints, she had a good sense of humour) and played with her children without the pretensions of a God, but she always protected them, even without their knowledge.

Once a rich man offered her tea in the nearby canteen, knowing that she used to drink tea frequently. Babajan agreed to go to the canteen with him, on condition that she would pay for the tea. At this, the proud rich man, in order to prove that he had a lot of money, shook his pockets and coins jingled. Babajan, without uttering even a word, accompanied him to the tea shop. After both of them had drunk tea, when the rich man wanted to make the payment, he was surprised to find that all the coins had vanished from his pocket. His ego was surely deflated and Babajan, seeing his pitiable situation, made the payment. When they returned to the neem tree, the visitor found the missing coins in his pocket. What Babajan preached, more by her actions than by words, was humility, truthfulness and service to all. She always advised people to be truthful at any cost.

Babajan used to cure people in her own way. Once she blew her breath on the eyes of a blind child while uttering something and instantaneously, the child got back her sight. She knew the past, present and future of everyone and everything. One night Babajan was found to be shouting excitedly, saying "It is fire. It is fire. Doors are locked and people are burning! Oh you fire, be extinguished." People could not understand what she was saying, till they came to know on the next day that a theatre in a small town known as Talegaon, situated at a distance of about twenty miles from Pune, had caught fire. As the theatre was full to capacity and the public from outside was pressing for entry, the authorities had locked the theatre. When the fire broke out, the people tried desperately to break the locks and surprisingly, the locks gave way quickly. Although some people died in the melee, many escaped death. It was established that Babajan was shouting "Fire, fire" at Pune just at the time when the fire had actually broken out at the theatre. The fire was brought under control quickly, thanks to the divine intervention of Babajan from a distance, as she had the power to control nature. Like Sainath, she would be found at times, talking loudly with invisible powers, asking them not to inflict pain on her children. Day in and day out, people would come to her and get both temporal and spiritual benefit. With the passage of time, the grand lady of love became a legend. Realising her stature among the public, the Cantonment Board built a shade for her, attached to the neem tree. Her abode was an open place, as she had nothing called privacy from her children.

It was autumn of the year 1931. The old matriarch had reached the age of about 110 years or more, ripe in age and ripe in her evolution process to meet the beloved (God), as the Sufis say. Due to frequent attacks of fever, her body became progressively weak. At times she remained in a state of supine immobility for days. Anticipating her end, a group of Muslims approached her to get permission to erect a *dargah* (tomb) for her at a certain place. She heard their request and suddenly flew into a rage. She asked, "How can the dead show concern for the living?" Whether requested by the ordinary people or the Cantonment Board authorities, she never agreed to leave the neem tree.

Her day of final departure came on 21st of September, 1931. Till the last day, she maintained her routine of distributing food to her children and blessing them. Her mortal body was entombed under the neem tree, after it was carried in the most historic procession Pune has ever witnessed. A marble tomb was built at the neem tree, which people visit today to get blessing and solace. No doubt she earned it. Her original name was Gulrukh. History remembers her as Babajan. Babajan means Baba (father) and Jan (soul). She was worshipped by many as father and others as mother, just like Shri Saibaba (God-father) and also Saimauli (God-mother). Whatever people called her, she was in a state which is beyond the dualities of nature - she was the realised one in the 'beyond' state.

Sarmad

Sarmad

- Birth details unknown; was a Jew by origin and came from Palestine.

- Was known to be a businessman selling Persian rugs and dry fruits in India during the reign of Emperor Shahjahan (1627 – 1658).

- Received his Divine Call on one of his visits to Patna, Bihar.

- Thereafter gave up His business in search of God and started living in India.

- As his fame spread, Emperor Shahjahan appointed Him as a tutor to his son.

- Around 1658, Aurangzeb ascended the throne, and Sarmad's conspirators got a new lease of life.

- Was ordered to be given capital punishment for moving around naked, but Aurangzeb was stunned by Sarmad's miracles.

- Was beheaded for declaring himself as "Anal Haq" (I am God).

Sarmad — The God-Intoxicated One

N ot many people, even in India, know about Sarmad, the perfect spiritual Master (*Sadguru*) of the 17th century. His tomb stands today near the Jama Masjid, Delhi, and is worshipped by those who know about the supreme sacrifice of this Master. A Jew by origin, Hazrat Saeed Sarmad came to India for carrying out trade between Palestine and, later, Armenia and India during the reign of Emperor Shahjahan (1627-1658). He sold Persian rugs and dry fruits in India and took home Indian gold, silver, cotton and textiles. Originally, he belonged to an affluent family with caring family members and rich friends. Trade with India made him very prosperous and life was smooth.

No one knows the ways of the Creator. As to how and when He draws someone towards Him is beyond the comprehension of the human intellect. Even Sarmad was not aware of it when he received His call. On one of his business quests he once went to Patna in Bihar. There he met an exceptionally good-looking young man. A strange thought occurred to him seeing this man — if such a humble creation of God could be so beautiful, how beautiful would God Himself be? If only he could see that majestic and beautiful God! Soon he became obsessed with the idea of seeing God face-to-face. Gradually this fascination became his only aim in life. He started searching for his beautiful God, whom he called his beloved (like the Sufis) and wandered wherever he could go. His search took him to remote and humble villages, crowded cities, serene river-banks, thick forests and desolate mountains in India. To get an answer which would satisfy his soul, he went through the religious scriptures of Hindus, Muslims and other religions. He observed the religious practices of various religions. He met religious teachers, but nobody could give him the answer. His divine thirst was not quenched. Slowly his business activities shrank to a minimum. At a later stage he could not carry on his business any longer. His only activity was his constant search for the beloved. Initially, his family members, relatives and friends tried to help him out of such a situation. However, all of them deserted him when he refused to return to the worldly enticements they all valued so much. He was left alone in India, a pauper, in an unknown and unfamiliar country. He walked alone, talked to himself and continued his search for the beloved. What he ate, what he wore, what he heard others telling him, where he slept, all became things of little concern to him. The path to the realisation of God has always been a painful one, requiring total surrender of anything and everything one possesses, coupled with suffering from the gross world from which the seeker tries to separate. The same people who were once friendly, knowing him to be a rich merchant, now started condemning him as a madman. He suffered all the humiliations quietly. At this stage, *Rubaiyat* (a form of poetry) started flowing from his agonised heart:

> "False is all earthly work, all vanity and mockery,
> But it fills the cup of transgressions to overflowing.
> The world laughs at me when I weep and pray and fast,
> While it indulges in empty rites."
> (*Rubaiyat* of Sarmad)

In this state of mind, Sarmad entered the God-intoxicated condition which spiritual seekers in advanced stages undergo. History has shown that when such a stage is reached by a seeker, God, in the form of a Perfect Master, appears to guide the neophyte. Sarmad met Bhikha, a famous saint of eastern Uttar Pradesh — his Perfect Master (*Sadguru*), who asked him to search for God inside him and not in the outside world. All saints and spiritual masters are unequivocal on the role of the Perfect Master. Without the grace of the Master, none can advance in the spiritual path beyond a certain point. The grace of the Master brought in both subtle and drastic changes in Sarmad. His Master virtually held his hand and led him to that stage of nothingness, where a man does not seek the splendours of God but only God Himself. Life after life, the *Sadguru* watches the birth and death cycles of his disciples going through *samskaras* (series of pains and pleasures). At the propitious moment He reveals himself to the disciple in the astral form or even in a physical form. There is no love like the Master's love. Whereas a touchstone can turn any ordinary stone to a piece of gold, the Master can bring up the disciple not merely to the stage of gold, but to the stage of the touchstone (i.e. to his own level). Sarmad's ardent prayer to his Master runs thus:

"O Master, shut not Thy door of clemency and grace
Upon him whom Thou hast accepted.
A weakling like myself cannot shoulder a heavy burden.
I have grown old and I pray to Thee, to save me from further transgressions."

(*Rubaiyat* of Sarmad)

The contact with the Master took away whatever little interaction Sarmad had with the outside world. He lost all sense of his gross body and walked around naked, unmindful of the ridicule and humiliation showered on him by the people.

Unaffected, he started spreading the message of love among the poor and the disenchanted ones. He pleaded with all to love only God and His creations and not money, wealth or fame. Gradually people started realising that even if Sarmad was naked from 'without', he was very rich with divine grace from 'within'. The people now started realising that there was fragrance in his madness, which gave joy to the hearts of those that approached Him. Sarmad would sit on the steps at the foot of Jama Masjid and tell people to follow his madness, as it was the only wisdom :

"The madness of the heart is the height of wisdom;
The confusion of love is beyond logic's comprehension
Can an ocean be contained in a small Jar?
Can the Master be God? Can a man be Lord?
They say it is imagination; let them say so. "

(*Rubaiyat* of Sarmad)

His name spread far and wide. Emperor Shahjahan also realised the worth of the saint and approached him to be the tutor to his first son, Dara Shikoh. Sarmad not only became the *Guru* to the heir-apparent of the Mughal empire, he also became the *Guru* of the distressed, the poor and miserable people of Delhi and surrounding areas.

Whosoever approached him was helped by him, irrespective of religion, caste and temporal status, for nature had endowed Sarmad with vast powers, which no king could ever possess. Like Kabir, he spoke openly against the superficial religious rites and preaching dished out by the *maulvis* and *sadhus* to the gullible people:

"O Sadhu, This robe of thine covers the sacred thread;
'Tis a deception involving struggle unending.
Carry not this burden of shamefulness on thy shoulder,
Then wilt thou avoid a thousand sufferings."

(*Rubaiyat* of Sarmad)

The simple hearts of the common and poor people of Delhi and around were touched by this direct appeal of love. They listened to him and hailed him as the new Messiah. His words echoed in their souls. They came in hundreds. They came in thousands. He helped all of them, for he took them as his own. His influence over the common mass was growing everyday. His popularity offended the religious leaders, the *maulvis*, *kazis* and *pandits*, who became jealous of his mass following. They declared him to be an infidel, leading the people away to spiritual doom. They started a series of conspiracies to annihilate him. However, they could do nothing as long as Shahjahan remained the Mughal emperor.

With the ascension of Aurangzeb (1658 AD) to the throne, the conspirators got a new lease of life. The Chief *Kazi* requested Aurangzeb to award capital punishment to Sarmad for moving about naked, which is a grave offence as per Islamic law. Nakedness comes in a very high stage of spiritual evolution, when the adept has lost the sense of his own body, engrossed in the God-experience. The naked saint remains in the state of a child, pure and natural, in the lap of nature (*Prakriti*). He has no will of his own but allows the course of nature or the will of God to guide him. He is always immersed in God (*Sat-Chit-Ananda* experience) remaining in a state of *Nirvikalpa Samadhi*. Gajanan Avdhoot, the famous saint of Maharashtra and many others, used to remain in such a state for years.

However, appreciation of such a divine state was beyond the comprehension of the jealous religious leaders and the law enforcers. The *kazis* and the *maulvis* conspired, and one Friday brought Aurangzeb to Jama Masjid, where Sarmad was lying naked. Aurangzeb requested Sarmad to cover himself with a blanket lying near him. Sarmad told Aurangzeb to spread the blanket over him, if he so liked. As Aurangzeb tried to unfold the blanket, he saw the most amazing scene of his life. He saw the chopped-off heads of his brothers, cousins and nephews who had been beheaded under his orders, rolling down from the fold of the blanket. Red blood was dripping from the heads. He was shocked and dropped the blanket in horror. Sarmad asked Aurangzeb whether he should use the blanket to cover his own physical nakedness or to cover Aurangzeb's moral nakedness. Without uttering a single word Aurangzeb went away, stunned and baffled. After this incident, for some time there was a lull.

However, the conspirators continued with their sinister design, if not openly. In the meantime, Sarmad had further progressed in his spiritual path and had almost reached the highest spiritual stage of calling himself God, *Anal-Haq* or *Brahmoshmi* (I am God). This gave a fresh opportunity to the conspirators. They charged him with violating the preaching of the *Quran* by calling himself God. This time they prevailed upon the Emperor to hold an inquiry into the charges personally. Aurangzeb, sitting in the court in the Red Fort, asked Sarmad if he had anything to say. Sarmad readily agreed to the charges made against him without any pleadings. Thereupon, Aurangzeb, as per the Islamic law, awarded capital punishment — Sarmad was to be beheaded the following day. Sarmad, on hearing the judgement, thanked Aurangzeb and God and said "Look, how merciful is my beloved. I was having a painful headache. Now the headache would be over." Resentment ran wild against this judgement of the Emperor. The people of Delhi loved Sarmad and he loved them. He was their father, mother, friend and spiritual guide. He gave them solace and help, both temporal and spiritual, in their distress, which all the authority of the Emperor could not provide.

As a precautionary measure, the next day, the army was posted everywhere in Delhi to contain the public upsurge. On the next day, at the appointed time, Sarmad was taken to a spot near the Jama Masjid. Thousands of people arrived to have a last look at their Master. There was no trace of pain on his face. He was calm and greeted everyone who went near him with a smile. When the executioner came to execute the orders, Sarmad, with a smile, and in a voice full of love, said "O God, you have come to me today in this form?" When he was being beheaded, he continued to say "Anal-Haq", (I am God). Then followed the most amazing scene the people of Delhi have ever seen. In the presence of a few thousand people, the beheaded body stood up and, carrying the head in one hand went up the steps of Jama Masjid, all the time saying "Anal-Haq" (I am God). The crowd was stunned at this spectacle; people cried loudly and shouted against Aurangzeb. The army could contain them with great difficulty. At that time Sarmad's Master, Bhikha appeared in an astral form and told Sarmad that his role in the gross body was over. Sarmad obeyed his Master. Thereafter the body immediately dropped.

According to another version, after the beheading, the body of Sarmad carried the head in one hand and started walking up the steps of Jama Masjid saying "Lahililah" (there is no God, but one God). At this stage, Sarmad for the first time recited the whole *Kalma* of the *Quran* as he had seen that one God — the supreme God. In the earlier stages he would only recite *Lahillah* (there is no God). In fact this half-recitation of the *Kalma* was considered an offence by the overtly jealous *maulvis* and *kazis*. It is also said that Sarmad's beheaded body proceeded towards Jama Masjid to ask Allah for divine justice. At this time his *Sadguru* appeared in an astral form and asked him to refrain from such an act, as it would bring about the instant death of Aurangzeb and the

Mughal empire. He asked Sarmad to allow nature to take its own course. Sarmad then submitted to the course of nature and the body fell down.

This then was Sarmad, one of the greatest spiritual martyrs that history has ever witnessed. Sarmad gave away his life deliberately, although he had all the powers for his protection. Saints at this level, being one with God, possess all the powers of God. They are beyond the trap of *Maya* (the life and death cycle) and have the power to control nature itself. Sarmad must have laughed within himself when Aurangzeb gave orders for his beheading. One of his *Rubaiyats* written much before his physical death, indicates how his end would come:

"Sarmad lies intoxicated with the love of the beloved,

Lost to everything, his cup is filled with the wine of love.

No terror of the executioner's sword can make him forsake his love.

Thus doth he reach unity with the Universal Soul."

Sarmad's agony lay not in being beheaded, but in his separation from his beloved. The God-intoxicated ultimately found his place in Him, after snapping the last link with the gross world that is, by his physical death, which he welcomed.

"I seek not the world; everything here is futile.

Without the treasure of seeing the beloved,

This is but a cage for me.

My only wish is to be one with Him,

If He be in the house a single word is enough."

Shri Akkalkot Maharaj

Shri Akkalkot Maharaj

- Birth details unknown, but is said to have wandered in many holy places in the Himalayas, Puri, Jagannath, Varanasi, Pandharpur, Nrisimhavadi, Mangalvedha, etc.

- First appeared on a Wednesday in the month of Aswin (Sept/Oct) in the year 1856 at Akkalkot and stayed there for nearly 22 years.

- In 1838 the Swami reached Mangalvedha and lived there for 12 years.

- In 1850 he departed from Mangalvedha and stayed in a place called Mohol for nearly 5 years and after wandering a Little, came to Sholapur.

- Around 1856 the Swami reached Akkalkot and stayed at the Khandoba Temple. He dined at the house of Cholappa.

- In 1857 the Kodak Photographic Company photographed the Swami for the first time, and found the presence of a big halo in the photograph.

- Between 1857 – 1878, he performed several miracles and gave spiritual guidance to many disciples and religious persons such as Shri Bidkar Maharaj, Shri Narasimha Saraswati, Shri Seetharam Maharaj, Yavan Aulia, Shri Anandanath Maharaj, Shri Balappa Maharaj, etc.

- Merged into the Banyan Tree ("Mula Purusha") in the month of Chaitra (April /May) in 1878.

Shri Akkalkot Maharaj —
The Dattatreya Incarnation

B elieved to be an incarnation of Shri Dattatreya
Avdhoot, the name of this spiritual master,
popularly called 'Swami Samarth', is a household
word in Maharashtra and the region around. As this *Sadguru*
chose to reside at a place called Akkalkot for 22 years, where
he attained *Mahasamadhi* in 1878, he is also known as the
'Maharaj of Akkalkot'. Akkalkot is situated in the Solapur
district of Maharashtra.

For the devotees of Shri Shirdi Sai Baba, it would be
inspiring to learn about the life and deeds of Swami Samarth.
A comparative picturisation of the lives of these two great
saints, i.e. Swami Samarth and Shri Sai Baba of Shirdi would
establish a surprising amount of commonness in their lives
and deeds, which include their methods of teaching, the
universality of their approach and the miracles they performed.
In fact, to say that they had many things in common would
be an understatement. Even a critical approach by a non-
conformist would ultimately lead to the assertion that the
overall role of these two spiritual masters during the second
half of the nineteenth century was similar, if not the same.
One who is capable of making finer spiritual analysis, would
be faced with a bewildering reality. The reality is that Swami
Samarth and Shri Shirdi Sai Baba were the manifestations of
the same Divine spirit in two gross bodies. Many published

writings on both these saints by different writers authenticate the interaction between these two *Sadgurus*, both in the gross and the subtle planes. Just before *Mahasamadhi*, Swami Samarth advised one of his disciples to worship Shri Sai at Shirdi, saying that he (Swami Samarth) would stay at Shirdi in future.

The early life of Swami Samarth, like that of Shri Shirdi Sai Baba, is shrouded in mystery. Mystical possibilities about his advent in the physical form have been conjectured by some writers. However, concrete proof, based on material evidence is lacking to authenticate such a theory. For that matter, even the facts regarding Shri Shirdi Sai Baba's advent and early life have not been established. Yet it does not really matter for those who have faith in Him and continue to experience his benevolence in different ways. How does it matter if Christ was born of a virgin mother! He took the pain of the suffering humanity and led them in the path of spirituality. This is what the world needs.

Shri Narasimha Saraswati, about three centuries before the advent of Swami Samarth, is believed to have been the earlier incarnation of Shri Dattatreya. The *Guru Charita* gives a lot of information about him. As per the most popular belief, Shri Narasimha Swami, after helping and spiritually uplifting a large number of people over a few decades, went away to the Himalayas for penance and went into *Samadhi*. In that state he remained for about three hundred years. With the passage of time a huge ant hill grew over him and he was lost to the outside world. One day a wood-cutter's axe accidentally fell on the bushes growing around the anthill. He was shocked to find bloodstains on the blade of the axe. He cleared the anthill and, lo and behold, he found a *Yogi* in meditation. The *Yogi* slowly opened his eyes and consoled the dumbfounded wood-cutter, saying it was the Divine Will that he was to reappear in the world to resume his mission. This *Yogi*, in his new role came to be known as Swami Samarth.

Prior to his settlement at Akkalkot, Swami Samarth roamed far and wide. While moving in the Himalayan region, he visited China. Thereafter, he visited places like Puri, Banaras, Hardwar, Girnaz, Kathiawad and Rameswaram. Because of his mobility and sudden appearance and disappearance from place to place, he came to be known as 'Chanchal Bharti', i.e. a wandering *sadhu*. He also stayed at Mangalvedha, a town near Pandharpur in Solapur district, Maharashtra, which had been inhabited earlier by famous saints like Domojipant and Chokhamela. He came to Akkalkot in 1856, where he continued his physical existence for 22 years. He came to Akkalkot on the invitation of one Chintopant Tol and stayed at a place on the outskirts of the town. What we call miracles are the normal ways of functioning of the God-realised ones. The *Risaldar* of that area, a Muslim, wanted to test the Swami by offering him a *chilum* without tobacco and asking him to smoke. Swami Samarth started smoking the empty *chilum* after lighting it, as if nothing had happened. Realising that he was an advanced spiritual person, the *Risaldar* apologised and made arrangements for his stay in the house of one Cholappa. It is in this small house that Swami Samarth lived upto his last.

Soon, the name of Swami Samarth as a Spiritual Master spread all around and devotees came seeking his blessings. Many of his gestures and mystic statements, which he used to make cryptically, were not understood by the ordinary people, although their meaning became apparent later. He treated Muslims, Christians and Parsees alike. His kindness was always bestowed on the poor, needy and the people on the lowest rungs of society. Both Hindu and Muslim festivals like Dussehra and Moharram used to be celebrated by him.

Like Shri Shirdi Sai who was, at times, seen rubbing coins in his hand while taking the names of some of his devotees, Swami Samarth used to toy with metallic rings frequently. He used to give these to some devotees at random. The surprised receiver always used to find the picture of his Deity (*Ishta*) engraved on the ring. As in Shirdi, Thursday became a special day of celebration at Akkalkot.

Like Shirdi Sai Baba, Swami Samarth of Akkalkot was fond of mass feeding. Once, on his visit to a place called Rampur, food was cooked for 50 people by a devotee named Rawaji, to celebrate his visit. However, hearing the news of Swami Samarth's arrival, hundreds of people from the neighbouring villages started rushing to the village. Seeing such a large number of people at his doorstep, Rawaji became visibly panicky. Moved by his plight, Swami Samarth asked Rawaji to get some empty baskets. When the baskets were brought from the market, idols of all the deities like Khandoba, Annapurna, etc. were put in them and food like *chapatis* were piled over them. Rawaji and his wife were asked to carry these baskets and walk three times around the *tulsi* plant. After that, they were asked to serve food from these baskets to the guests without looking into them. When food was being served, Rawaji and his wife were amazed to see that the baskets were never exhausted, even after hundreds of people had been served. After all the people who had come finished their meal, Swami Samarth took his meal. This is known as 'Annapurna Sidhi.'

Swami Samarth had the capacity to read the minds of all the people coming to him and was also able to know about their past and future. Baba Saheb Jadhav, one of his great devotees, one day came to meet the Master. Seeing him, suddenly Swami Samarth said " Oh Potter! there is a summons coming in your name." The potter being a part of the close circle of Swami Samarth, understood the meaning of this sentence and begged of the Swami to save him from the approaching death, so that he could continue to serve him (the Master). Moved by his devotion, Swami Samarth looked up towards the sky and muttered something, as if he was addressing someone who was invisible. Suddenly, he pointed his hand towards a bull passing nearby and said in a loud voice " Go to the bull ." In the presence of a large number of devotees, the bull instantly fell dead. Jadhav, with a fresh lease of life, devoted himself totally to the service of Swami Samarth thereafter. Similarly, a European engineer from Solapur visited Swami with the earnest hope of having a son. As he approached Swami Samarth, the latter just looked at him and told him that he would have a son within a year. That is exactly what happened.

The *Sadgurus* or the Spiritual Masters always endeavour to change the quality of men that encounter them. Besides bestowing material benefit, they try to uplift them spiritually. Once a Jewish doctor, who was working as an eye specialist in the J.J. Hospital, Bombay met Swami Samarth. The doctor was very proud of his professional competence. Seeing him, Swami Samarth asked "Tell me Doctor, how many of the eye patients you have treated have lost their eyesight forever?" This sentence made a tremendous impact on the doctor. He realised that many people had lost their sight forever inspite of being treated by him. His ego immediately vanished and thereafter he became a devotee of Swami Samarth. After retirement, the doctor settled down at Akkalkot and served the Master till the last.

It is said that a touchstone can convert an ordinary metal to gold. The Spiritual Masters are such touchstones that they can convert an ordinary metal, not just to gold but to that of a touchstone. They are capable of giving spiritual life to any person in a fraction of a second by a touch, a look, a word or even by a mere thought. A person like Ramanand Bidkar, who had lived an immoral life for a long period, was made into a saint called Bidkar Maharaj by the kind grace of Swami Samarth, who by one look i.e. *Drishti Diksha* evolved him spiritually. Under his guidance, Shri Balappa Maharaj, Shri Gangadhar Maharaj, Shri Gajanan Maharaj and many others rose to spiritual eminence and contributed a lot to society.

After serving the poor, curing the sick and helping the spiritual seekers over a few decades, Swami Samarth one day suddenly announced that the time had come for him to go out of his physical existence. It was *Chaitra Sudha Trayodasi Shaka* 1800, i.e. 4 pm on a Tuesday in the year 1878 AD. At this time he seated himself in *Padmasana* (Lotus Posture) and uttered his last words - "No one should weep - I shall always be present at all places and I shall respond to every call of the devotees." Shri Sai Baba of Shirdi had also said exactly the same thing before His *Mahasamadhi.*

Just before he left his gross body, one devotee called Keshav Nayak who was emotionally charged, asked "Maharaj, since you are going, who will give us protection?" Swami Samarth gave him a pair of his sandals to worship. He told him "In future I will be staying at Shirdi in district Ahmednagar." Another devotee, Krishna Ali Bagkar decided to go to Akkalkot and worship the *padukas* of Swami Samarth.

Thereafter Swami Samarth appeared to him in a dream and told him "Now I am staying at Shirdi, go there and worship me." Bagkar went to Shirdi, where he stayed for six months. Later, when he wanted to take leave of Shri Sai and go to Akkalkot again, Shri Sai told him "What is there in Akkalkot, Maharaj of Akkalkot is staying here." Bagkar realised that there was no difference between Swami Samarth and Shri Sai Baba of Shirdi, as he recalled his earlier dream.

The divine game (*leela*) of Swami Samarth did not end with his *Mahasamadhi*. His devotees continue to experience the miracles of his visible and invisible help even today. It is exactly like the experiences of the devotees of Sai Baba of Shirdi after His *Mahasamadhi* in 1918. Many people have authenticated his appearance in physical form before them. These people are not only rural folk. Many of them are well-educated people like doctors, teachers, etc. For example, Dr. S.V. Marathe, a private medical practitioner of Pune, once underwent treatment in a chest hospital at a place called Aundh in 1964. Many of his friends were anxious to come and visit him. At this juncture, Swami Samarth appeared before many of his friends in a dream and gave the same message to all of them. He asked them not to worry about Dr. Marathe, as he was under his (Swami Samarth's) protection and also not to come to Aundh. Once, the doctor's monetary difficulties were miraculously solved when he prayed to Swami Samarth. Having solved the problems, Swami Samarth appeared in his dream and demanded his *dakshina* saying "Give me *pedas*," exactly the way Shri Sainath is famous for asking *dakshina*.

Hundreds of devotees continue to have miraculous experiences with the Perfect Master even today. But his miracles and those of Shri Sainath are so alike that one would be drawn to the conclusion that they are not two masters but are one and, perhaps, the ONLY ONE.

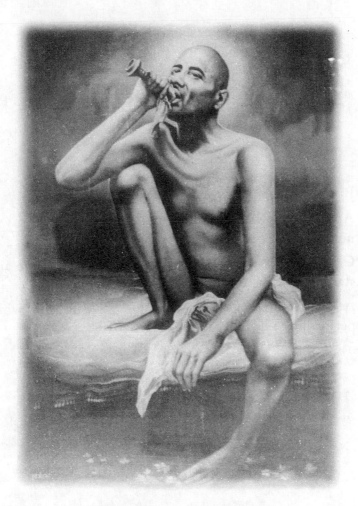

Shri Gajanan Avdhoot

Shri Gajanan Avdhoot

- Birth details unknown.

- Appeared at Shegaon on 23rd February 1878 and was noticed collecting leftover food in a garbage dump.

- Came to Bankatlal's house and began staying there and started His divine Leelas.

- Attained Samadhi on 8th September 1910 at 8 a.m while performing His pujas to the Lord.

Shri Gajanan Maharaj — The Avdhoot

There is hardly any authenticated information about the early life of Shri Gajanan Avdhoot, popularly known as Gajanan Maharaj. His place of birth, date of birth, parentage, etc. are shrouded in mystery, although people speculate that he was born in a place named Sajjangarh in Maharashtra. It has been observed that the terminal points (birth and death) in the lives of spiritually advanced souls is often mystical. For example, saints like Shri Gorakh Nath, Shri Sai Baba of Shirdi and also Shri Gajanan Avdhoot did not reveal their past and did not encourage people to enquire about it. Shri Gorakh Nath, one of the *Navnathas*, was found as a child on a heap of garbage. There are numerous unconfirmed stories about the birth of Shri Sainath.

However, Shri Gajanan Avdhoot was first noticed collecting leftover food items in a garbage dump on the outskirts of the village Shegaon in Maharashtra by a person named Bankatlal Agarwal. The Maharaj, although possessed of a shining and extremely healthy body, was at that time in a super-conscious state, without a sense of his own body (*Vid'eha*), for he had no clothes. Bankatlal, who had earlier associated with some spiritually advanced persons, sensed that the apparently crazy person collecting food from the dustbin might be a *Siddha*. It was 23rd February, 1878. Bankatlal, along with a friend named Damodar Pant Kulkarni, approached Maharaj with humility and asked "Maharaj, why are you eating leftover food? If you are hungry, I will certainly make arrangements for you." However, Maharaj paid no heed to his words and continued to eat his food in a state of utter detachment. Seeing this, Bankatlal ran to the ashram situated nearby, collected whatever food he could, and came back to Maharaj. As he offered food, Maharaj mixed up all the food items and gulped them down. It must be realised that saints at this level actually do not have a sense of taste, as they are in the 'beyond- the-body' state. Bankatlal, thereafter, went away to fetch some drinking water. By the time he returned, he was shocked to see the Maharaj happily drinking water from the water reservoir meant for cattle. Bankatlal was convinced that he was in the presence of no ordinary mortal, but a highly-evolved spiritual entity. He prostrated in reverence and asked for blessings. By the time he lifted his head, Maharaj had vanished from there.

Disappearance and reappearance is one of the eight *siddhis* that *yogis* of India used to possess in the past. Bankatlal was extremely sad and depressed at the sudden disappearance of Maharaj, but at that time, little did he know that Gajanan Avdhoot was his own *Sadguru*, who had himself come at that time. *Sadgurus* or Perfect Masters and *Qutabs* attract or reach their disciples when the appropriate time comes to lead them to their spiritual goal. Their attraction becomes so powerful that it becomes difficult for anyone to resist. Hence, it is not surprising that Bankatlal was so sad at his disappearance. His mind could think of nothing except Gajanan Avdhoot all the time, and he searched for him the whole day without any success. However, he again found Maharaj in the evening when he went to the old Shiva temple to join a *kirtan* party. He was overjoyed to find him and in an emotionally choked voice, requested Baba to come and stay in his house. Maharaj, on his request, came to his house, from where his divine function (*leela*) started.

The function of the *Sadguru* is to give a universal push to all the human beings and other species towards spiritual evolution. For them, caste, religion, sex, nationality and even difference in species, etc. do not matter. They are humans with human beings and animals with animals. When they start playing this role, people from far and wide start getting drawn, as if by the pull of an invisible force. In fact, this is what Shri Sainath used to say, "I draw my children from thousands of miles like a child pulling a bird with a string tied to its legs." With the advent of Gajanan Avdhoot, thousands of people from far and wide started flocking to Bankatlal's house, both for spiritual and temporal upliftment. With so many people visiting his house, Bankatlal tried to make whatever arrangements he could. It is not easy to have a Perfect Master as one's guest, as they are beyond all *gunas* (*sattwa*, *Rajo* and *tamma gunas*). They are not limited by social or religious laws. Whatever they say or think, happens as they only carry out the functions with the help of nature. Their behaviour at times becomes extremely unpredictable to the common man. At times they behave like children, at times like madmen or even like people possessed. Nevertheless whatever they do, it is for the good of others. Only spiritually advanced people can understand the motivation behind the actions of a *Sadguru*.

Maharaj often used to quietly escape from Bankatlal's house even at odd hours, without informing him about his destination. Poor Bankatlal used to search him out by strenuous efforts and would request him to come back. One day Maharaj quietly strayed to another village named Adgaon. At about midday, when the sun was at its zenith, he approached a farmer cultivating his land and requested for some drinking water. The farmer, named Bhaskar Patel, thought that he was one of the ordinary mendicant *sadhus* and started rebuking him, saying that he would not give a drop of water which he had carried from home to a *sadhu* who is a parasite in society. Maharaj only smiled without any reaction and slowly walked towards what looked like an old well. Bhaskar Patel again started testing him from behind, saying that it was a dry well, so how could anybody get water from there. Maharaj reached the well and meditated for a few moments, and soon the well which had been dry for about twelve years, was filled with clean water. He quenched his thirst with this water. Seeing this miracle, Bhaskar Patel realised that he (Maharaj) was no ordinary man and profusely apologised for his intemperate behaviour. The *Sadgurus* are oceans of love and mercy and they are incapable of being annoyed or angry or revengeful. That is why the epithets *Kripa Sindhu* or *Daya Nidhi*, etc. are used for them. Maharaj was moved seeing the plight of Bhaskar Patel and told him that he had created water for him in the well, so that Patel did not have to carry water from the village strenuously every day for cultivation or drinking. The love that we sometimes feel within us, the depth of kindness that stirs in our heart when we are in touch with a *Sadguru*, is because the *Sadguru* first showers his total love and compassion on us, without any qualification and even without asking. This is what is known as *Ahetuk Kripa*. Thus, by total sacrifice of himself, the *Sadguru* tries to evolve his children towards their goal and teaches that sacrifice for others without any intention of getting returns engenders godly qualities in human beings. The *Sadguru* teaches by his own example that anyone in order to shine should sacrifice himself. No one can truly help others without any sacrifice of himself.

Protection of the *Sadguru* is the strongest armoury in a person's life, because the extent to which a *Sadguru* can go to protect his children cannot be imagined. Shri Sai Baba of Shirdi, who left His body while protecting Tatya Patil is one such example. Once Maharaj, invited by Bankatlal, went to his farmland to eat cornstalk (*bhutta*). Baba, along with a group of devotees sat under a tree, lit a fire and started roasting the corn. Nobody had noticed that there was a beehive on the tree. As the smoke from the fire reached the hive, the honey-bees came out in swarms and started stinging everybody. Except Maharaj, all of the devotees ran away. All the honey-bees, thereafter, settled on the body of Maharaj, who continued to stay unmoved. Suddenly Bankatlal saw this from a distance and was moved by the plight of Maharaj. When he approached Maharaj to render help, Maharaj, addressing the honey-bees said "You go back to your own place. My dear devotee Bankatlal is coming this way. He should not have any pain." No sooner had he uttered these words than the entire swarm of honey-bees returned to the hive. The devotees on their return, saw that Baba's whole body was full of stings. Ordinarily, no person can quietly bear the stinging of a swarm of honey-bees. All of them started thinking that Maharaj must be in pain. Seeing their plight, Shri Gajanan Avdhoot gave a smile and took a deep breath. At once, all the stings fell out of his body in hundreds and the people were consoled. In this case what the *Sadguru* did was to take on his own body the pain of the stings, not allowing his children to suffer.

After a short stay at Khodgaon, the Maharaj returned to Shegaon. There he moved to the house of one Khandu Patil. His style of living was so ordinarily like that of Shri Sai Baba of Shirdi, that it was not easy for everyone to make out the depth of this spiritual personality at first. One day, about ten South Indian *Brahmins*, with the intention of earning some money, came to the house of Khandu Patil and started reciting the *Vedas* aloud. Maharaj, who was sleeping under the cover of a blanket, suddenly woke up during the rendition and pointed out to the *Brahmins* that they were pronouncing the *Vedas* in the wrong manner. Thereafter, he himself started reciting those portions of the *Vedas* which the *Brahmins* had wrongly recited. Soon the *Brahmins* realised that Maharaj was a saint of a very high spiritual order and prostrated at his feet. Maharaj blessed them all and also gave them *dakshina*.

One day Maharaj went to the Nilakanth temple near the village and desired to stay there. Patil built a leaf cottage for him and people started visiting the place. Once a group of *Gossains* (a type of *sadhu*), claiming to be the disciples of one Brahmagiriji, reached the place where Maharaj was staying. The pretentious *sadhus* demanded *halwa*, *puri* and *ganja* from Patil. They also told him that by doing so he would get more *punya* than by serving a mad and naked person like Gajanan Maharaj. After taking food and *ganja*, just in order to prove his superiority over Maharaj the group leader, Brahmagiriji, to draw the attention of the people, started lecturing on the *Gita*. He started explaining the verse "*Nainam-Chhindanti Sastrani, Nainam Dahanti Pabakah*" meaning, neither weapons can destroy the soul nor can fire burn it. Inspite of his best efforts, people were found to be collecting around Gajanan Maharaj, who was smoking his *chilum* sitting on a wooden bed right opposite Brahmagiriji. The latter's ego was hurt and he became very angry at the absence of proper public appreciation. Strange are the ways of the *Sadgurus*. In this situation a strange thing suddenly occurred.

The bed on which Maharaj was sitting suddenly caught fire. As the fire rose up, the disciples of Maharaj requested him to come out of the fire and also started arranging for water. Maharaj said that neither water would be used to extinguish the fire nor would he get out of the burning bed. Addressing Brahmagiriji who was enjoying the sight, Maharaj said, "Since you have been telling people for the last one hour that neither weapon can destroy nor fire can burn the soul, please come and prove it by sitting on the fire." Brahmagiriji did not react to this but tried to avoid the situation. Then Maharaj asked a physically strong disciple to catch hold of Brahmagiriji and bring him before Maharaj. One can well imagine the condition of a pretentious *sadhu* in such a situation. His ego was totally shattered and he repented, not only for his behaviour but also his pretentiousness. Maharaj pardoned him and advised him on the path to be followed for spiritual upliftment.

The *Sadguru* is the Universal *Guru*. He deals with each person at his level of consciousness. He tries to destroy the ego through his superior powers in order to evolve that person. All such limitations of mind and body that are not conducive to the evolution of a soul are removed by him slowly. What method in the gross, subtle or mental level the *Sadguru* may use can never be predicted by any one.

Hazrat Baba Tazuddin

Hazrat Baba Tazuddin

- Birth : 27th of January 1861 at Kamthi, Nagpur.

- Death of his father when he was barely a year old.

- Received divine blessings from Hazrat Abdulla Shah in his 6th year, who said "Prophet Mohammed has descended on you".

- Death of his mother when he was 9 years old.

- Joined the 13th Nagpur Regiment at the age of 20.

- In the year 1884, met the famous Chisti Saint Hazrat Dawood Shah and began meditating and Mujahedas (spiritual practices).

- Shortly thereafter, he resigned from the army.

- Admitted to a lunatic asylum on 26th August 1892.

- Was taken out of the asylum in 1908 by Maharaja Raghoji Rao and taken to the palace, ending his 16-year stay at the asylum.

- Between 1920 – 1925, Baba's reputation spread far and wide as the greatest Sufi saint of modern history, and manifold miracles of the highest order were experienced and recorded.

- His spirit merged with the Infinite on 17th August 1925.

Hazrat Baba Tazuddin

H azrat Baba Tazuddin was one of the five Perfect Masters (*Sadgurus*) of his age. Whereas Shri Sai Baba of Shirdi headed this group of five masters as *Param Sadguru*, the other masters were Babajan of Pune, Upasani Maharaj of Sakori (near Shirdi in Maharashtra) and Shri Narayan Maharaj of Keda Gaon (Maharashtra). Such is the play of nature known as *maya* (illusion) that this Perfect Master was declared a lunatic and kept in confinement in the Nagpur lunatic asylum for more than sixteen years. However, Baba Tazuddin started his divine play from this place and virtually converted the asylum to a place of worship.

Baba Tazuddin was born on the 21st of January in the year 1861 at a place called Kamthi, situated near Nagpur in the state of Maharastra. From birth itself, there was something unusual about the child, for the newborn baby would not cry at all. He would, at times, open his eyes and look at people and again go to sleep. All normal methods to induce the child to cry having failed, the parents took recourse to a traditional shock method of touching a hot iron to the forehead and ear of the child. With the application of this method, the child jerked out of his stupor and started crying. The burnt marks thus made on the head and ears of the child remained on his body till the last.

More often than not, it is seen that highly developed souls become orphans in their early childhood, so that they become free to operate in their spiritual world. This had happened with Shri Shirdi Sai and this also happened with Baba Tazuddin. His father expired when he was only one year old and his mother expired when he was only nine years old. The care of this orphan was taken over by his maternal grand-mother and maternal uncle Abdul Rahman. As a child, Baba started his education at the age of six in a local *madarsa* in Kamthi. During this time a spiritually-developed soul, known as Hazrat Abdulla Shah, visited the *madarsa* and saw the child Tazuddin. He immediately told the teacher "Why are you teaching this child? He has got all knowledge from his past life." Saying this, he took out a dry fruit (*khumani*) from his bag, ate half, and put the other half in the mouth of the child saying, "Eat less, sleep less and speak less. Read *Quran* XXX."

As soon as the child ate the dry fruit, God-consciousness dawned on him and for about three days he remained in a state of spiritual ecstasy, shedding tears in secluded places. Obviously Hazrat Abdulla Shah had given Tazuddin the spiritual powers or consciousness known as *Shaktipata* in the Hindu *Yoga* system. Thereafter, the child was found to be always in a state of contemplation in secluded places.

At the age of 18, the financial condition of his maternal uncle deteriorated due to floods. As a result, both Baba and his maternal uncle searched for a job. In 1881, at the age of 20, Baba joined the Nagpur Army Regiment. Soon a contingent of the regiment, where Baba was serving, was sent to a place called Sagar. At Sagar, Baba used to manage his duties as an army sepoy, somehow spending the best of the time in doing *namaz* and contemplation. Most of the nights he used to spend with a highly developed spiritual soul known as Hazrat Baud Saheb, undergoing spiritual practices. Hazrat Baud Saheb is, therefore, recognised as one of the spiritual masters of Tazuddin Baba. His absence from the army camp at nights, and his least regard for the service created problems from the higher authorities. One day, in an intoxicated state, Baba suddenly submitted his resignation from the army and left the camp.

He then roamed around in the streets of Sagar like a mad man, without any sense of body. Soon his maternal grandmother heard the news and took him away to Kamthi . She tried to get him cured through doctors and *hakims* thinking that he was mad. The doctors and *hakims* could hardly improve his condition, as Baba Tazuddin's consciousness had by that time, transcended the gross and subtle body and was floating in the vast ocean of divine consciousness — beyond multiplicism and duality of nature. As has befallen the destiny of many spiritual seekers, children started throwing stones at him, to which he would never react. The people around him discarded him as useless for their purpose and declared him mad and therefore, humiliated him whenever and wherever they could. However, miracles also started taking place around him. He would suddenly tell people about their past and warn them about future problems. One day in that *Videha* state (beyond body state) he approached a British woman in a naked state. The horrified woman complained to the army authorities about such uncivilised behaviour. An army officer caught hold of him and got him admitted in the lunatic asylum of Nagpur on the 26th of August 1892. This is one of the biggest illusions of Nature (*maya*) as I see it: the mad people of the mad world declaring the knowledge-incarnate, who come to redeem them of their worldly madness, as mad. But how could the authorities confine a soul that is in a state of pure consciousness, within the four walls of a lunatic asylum? As was the practice, the inhabitants of the asylum used to be locked up in barracks and cells at night. Similarly, Baba was also put in confinement under strict vigil.

Soon after he was locked up in the asylum, a strange incident took place that spread Baba's name far and wide. Baba was admitted in the asylum on 26th August 1892. On the same day many people saw him moving freely in the streets of Kamthi, even after he was locked up. On the next day i.e. 27th an army sepoy, who, under the orders of the magistrate, had brought Baba to the lunatic asylum the previous day, saw Baba roaming in the streets. The shocked sepoy ran back and informed the British officer of the regiment, about it. The officer immediately mounted his horse and searched for Baba. He ultimately found him sitting under a tree smiling at him. The British officer was so enraged at seeing him moving freely that he straightaway rode to the lunatic asylum at Nagpur, situated at half-an-hour distance from Kamthi. He asked the doctor on duty "Where is that insane whom I sent here yesterday ?" The doctor informed him that he was in a locked room and also showed the officer the room where Baba was locked. Lo and behold, the officer found that Baba Tazuddin was sitting inside the room, in the same posture in which he had seen him sitting under the tree only half an hour ago, smiling at him. On seeing the officer, Baba said, "Brother, you are doing your work and I am doing my work." The officer was so influenced by the divine personality of Baba that he instantly became his disciple and started visiting Baba every Sunday with his family members. Thereafter the asylum authorities were agreeable to Baba moving around inside the asylum compound and outside. Gradually, Baba's name became so famous that thousands of people from near and far started lining up before the lunatic asylum every day, seeking Baba's *darshan*, blessings and help. During his 16-year stay in the asylum, Baba cured thousands of people of diseases, granted children to the childless and took on his shoulders the responsibilities (both temporal and spiritual) of lakhs of his devotees.

Miracles are the ways of functioning of the Masters. Since, more often, they work through the subtle and mental mediums than in the gross, ordinary mortals term them as miracles. The forces creating miracles are subtle forces of nature that have not yet been discovered. Since the work of the Perfect Masters precipitates hundreds and thousands of actions at different places at the same time, they employ the subtle methods. Those who have become mediums of miracles know for sure that there are definite principles on which the so-called miracles operate. For them they are not miracles, but a normal way of functioning at their level of consciousness.

There was a devotee called Shri Narain Rao Kamalkar, who used to visit Baba daily in the asylum. On a Monday, he decided to see Baba in the asylum and then visit the temple of Lord Shiva. When he reached Baba, he was shocked to find a snake hanging around the neck of Baba. He ran to Dr. Abdul Mazid, and informed him about the incident. Both hurried back and found the snake still around Baba's neck. Baba told them "Why are you afraid? Come in." By the time they had opened the lock and entered, the snake had vanished from Baba's neck. Looking at the stunned Narain Rao, Baba asked "Why do you want to have more *darshan*?" In a voice choked with emotion Narain Rao cried "Baba, whose *darshan* shall I have now? You are my Shiva."

The Perfect Masters are not confined by any religion, any creed , caste or even by scriptural injunctions or prescribed methods of worship, etc. They are in a state of *Swechchachara* which means acting by total 'free will' without any limitations of nature. This is not to be understood as *Durachara* which is the negative state of assertion of free will. Baba's fame and love for people had been drawing thousands of people daily to the lunatic asylum. Even the staff of the asylum, including the doctors were his devotees. The doctor gave a report that

Baba was not mad but was a person of unusual qualities which medical science cannot explain. In the meantime, Maharaja Bahadur Shrimant Raghoji Rao Bhonsle, the Maharaja of Nagpur, had become an ardent devotee of Baba and started visiting him regularly. One day, in the evening, he thought of getting Baba released from the lunatic asylum and bringing him to his palace at Shakardara. The same night, he saw a vision in which Baba appeared and pointing towards a red palace, said "Oh, elder brother, let me stay here." It was the early morning (3.00 AM) of 9th July 1908, a Thursday. The Maharaja immediately called his officials and discussed the steps to be taken to get Baba released. The council decided that an application for release should be immediately made by the Maharaja to the Governor, Central provinces. Ultimately after depositing a sum of two thousand rupees as security, the Maharaja secured the release of Baba on the 21st of September 1908 and brought him to his palace. From his palace Baba started his divine work known as *leela*.

Once Baba was lying down on the sands of the river Kanhan when two ladies by the name of Shantabai and Subhadrabai from Amaravati , approached him. While touching the feet of Baba they mentally prayed to him for children, as they were childless. The omniscient (*Pragyan Ritambhara*) Baba heard their inner prayers and gave a *laddoo* to each after tasting them himself. He blessed them. While they were returning, Shantibai ate the *laddoo* as a *prasad*, but Subhadrabai did not because Baba had tasted the *laddoo* and was a Muslim by birth. She quietly got the *laddoo* buried in the sand. As the divine will would have it, Shantibai got a son nine months later. When the child was about two months old, she came to Baba with the child for his blessings. Subhadra, who had not conceived even by that time, accompanied her. When Shantibai put her child at the feet of Baba, Subhadra could not control herself.

She fell at the feet of Baba, and cried "Baba where is my child?" Baba told her to seek the child from beneath the sand (indicating he knew where the *laddoo* was). Subhadrabai immediately realised her mistake and repented profusely before Baba. The Perfect Masters are incarnations of kindness. Baba was moved by her repentance and plight. He blessed her that she would have a son which she got after a year. The Perfect Master is a wish-fulfilling tree (*Kalpabriksha*) who even showers unconditional grace (*Ahetuk Kripa*).

A poor scheduled caste woman called Tara once wished to feed Baba, but since Baba was staying in the palace, Tara did not know how to approach him, and was afraid that some people may not take it kindly. So, she cooked the food and tied it in a piece of cloth to a *jamun* tree near the palace. Sometime later, people from high classes kept the best of dishes before Baba for his lunch. Baba said "I will not eat all these. Get me the food tied in the *jamun* tree". Everybody started searching but could not find the food. Ultimately Baba got up from his seat, brought the food from the tree and ate only that with utter satisfaction. The Perfect Masters are hungry not for the food offered by people, but for the love behind such offerings.

A man called Shri Hanumant Rao, an employee of the State Secretariat, was so devoted to Baba that one day he had thought of becoming a Muslim so that he could be closer to Baba. No sooner had this thought flashed in his mind than Baba who was sitting nearby, generally asked everyone around him to give him a book. Incidentally, Hanumant Rao had a concise *Gita* in his pocket. On hearing Baba's words he handed over the book to him. Baba took the book, opened a page and looking at Hanumant Rao, said "I stay in this Book." Rao at once understood the meaning of Baba's words and started crying in spiritual ecstasy. The spiritual masters never encourage anyone to change his religion. They only see the theme of humanism which is the basis of all religions.

There was a prostitute by the name of Giriji, who was a devotee of Baba. Suddenly, she caught some disease and remained ill for long. Another devotee of Baba, Kashinath Patel, one day sent a person to the house of Giriji to enquire about her health. That man came and found Giriji dead and informed Kashinath accordingly. Kashinath directed him to go and ask Tazuddin Baba whether to bury the body of Giriji or to burn it.

On his way to Baba's place, he found a close attendant of Baba carrying tea in a pot. In the course of their conversation, Patel's man told the attendant of Baba that Giriji was dead. When Baba's attendant heard that Giriji was dead, he told the other person that Baba had asked him to ensure that Giriji drank the tea. Therefore, he insisted on carrying the tea to Giriji. Both of them reached Giriji's house and found her body surrounded by women. The attendant of Baba, said in a loud voice "Giriji, *Hazur* has sent tea for you. Take it." He repeated the sentence three times. After the third time Giriji opened her mouth and a little tea was poured in. After taking the tea, she came back to life and lived for a few years more.

The love of a Perfect Master for his devotees is somewhat like, but more than, the love of the mother towards the child. Whosoever surrenders to him, finds that he takes care of his biggest and even smallest problems. Since his words are the ultimate truth, whatever he promises is fulfilled, even after he has left his body. Let us see one example. Sometimes, Baba used to travel in a horse-driven cart to distant places. One devotee named Hiralal, used to be his driver. When Baba once declared that he would leave his body in a few days (he left his body on the 17th of August 1925), Hiralal started crying. He asked Baba "*Hazur*, under whose protection are you leaving us and going?" Baba told him "You always stay in front of me (the driver sits at the front in a horse cart) and I will always stay behind you."

It so happened that in 1965, on the day of *Moharram*, the annual procession i.e. Baba's *Tazia* started from Baba's place which was now named Tazabaad, and moved towards the main square (called Jhad Square) with people shouting "*Allah ho Akbar*". Suddenly the people carrying the *Tazia* heard the cry "*Ram naam satya hai*" from another procession moving in front of them. Those who knew what Baba had told Hiralal during his last days, were astounded to find that the procession in the front was carrying the dead body of Hiralal. Tears rolled down from their eyes when they saw Hiralal's body going in front and Baba's *Tazia* following — a promise kept by Baba forty years after his departure. One of the main functions of a *Sadguru* is to stand by his devotees at the time of their death, in gross or subtle form, to lead the soul towards further evolution. No one else, i.e. no other *Guru*, parents, relatives, or even *yogis* has the power to render such help to the souls once they have left the body.

By 1925, Baba had completed his 64th year. In the month of August his health started deteriorating. Maharaja Raghoji Rao pressed the best doctors into service, but no doctor could cure Baba, who had himself decided about his departure. Raghoji Rao understood that Baba was getting ready to depart. He asked Baba to allow people to have *darshan* even if medical advice did not permit. The ever-benevolent Baba just smiled and agreed. As the news spread, thousands of people came to the king's palace and had the last *darshan* of their beloved master, who had served and protected them for decades. The stream of visitors continued till the last moment of Baba's departure on 17th August 1925. On that Monday, Baba lifted his hand in blessing to all, looked at them lovingly and them quietly laid his body on the bed. By the time doctors could check him, the *Shivatma* had already left the gross body for its universal abode. But, today the experiences of people visiting the *Samadhi* of Baba establishes the truth that the Perfect Masters always exist, in whatever form, in the time continuum, for they are in the 'beyond' state.

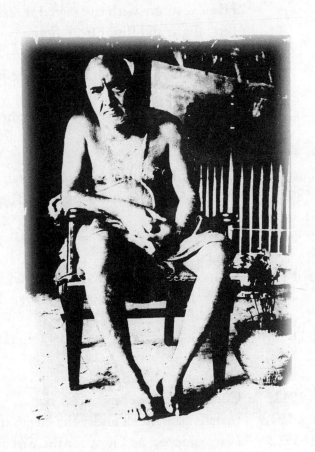

Shri Upasani Maharaj

Shri Upasani Maharaj

15th May 1870	Birth of Kashinath Govind Upasani Sastri.
1877	His investiture with the sacred thread.
1884	First flight and flight from home.
1885	First wife's death and second marriage.
1886	Second flight from home and frequent flights subsequently.
1890	Visit to Kalyan and state of trance at Bhorgad cave.
21st July 1890	Returns to Satana.
8th August 1890	Death of His father on Gokulashtami.
1892 – 1895	Studies Ayurveda and Sanksrit and begins practice.
1896-1905	Practises medicine at Amraoti and Nagpur.
10th April 1910	Starts on pilgrimage to Omkareshwar, has respiration problems and a miraculous escape.
April 1911	Starts in quest of yogis to cure respiratory troubles.
27th June 1911	First visit to Shirdi.
6th Feb. 1912	Composes arti verses on Sai Baba.
10th Aug. 1912	Installs Saipaduka under the Neem tree.
18th July 1913	Is worshipped as Guru for the first time under Sai Baba's order.
1914 – 1917	Visits Shindi, Nagpur, Shirdi and Poona and then settles at Sakuri.
22nd Dec. 1941	Visits His birth place Satana for the last time and installs 12 Jyotirlingas with His own hands.
24th Dec. 1941	Attains Mahasamadhi at Sakuri.

Shri Upasani Maharaj —
The Loftiest Creation of
Shri Sainath

A n explanation about the role and greatness of Shri
Sai of Shirdi would remain incomplete without
the understanding of the life of Kashinath Govind
Upasani Sastri, who later came to be known as 'Shri Upasani
Maharaj'. Shri Sai's life was full of miracles, but the greatest
miracle was His elevation of this once inconsequential person
to the status of a *Sadguru* within a period of four years! The
methods used by Shri Sai to completely transform Kashinath
Sastri, the pains taken by Him to protect the neophyte and
the assurance with which He nurtured this unsure and
confused disciple to the state of a Perfect Master, would
indicate the place of Shri Sai in the spiritual hierarchy of this
world.

Born on 5th May, 1870 at Satana, Maharashtra (in India),
Kashinath did not exhibit traits of a normal child from the
beginning, although his deviations did not indicate the
existence of any super-intelligence or excellence in him. He
held extremely strong views about two vital aspects of life
when in his teens. First, he declared that the formalised
educational learning was only for bread-winning and,
therefore, after doing three years in a vernacular elementary
school he left it: merciless caning by his teacher being the

immediate cause of his action. Secondly, he hated and condemned the body (i.e. his own body) as the creator of limitations and pain in life. He spent all his time doing *asanas* (exercises of *Yoga*), *pranayama* (breath control exercises), repetition of mantras, etc. With such an attitude he could earn nothing and for his family members he was a problem child. To make matters worse, his family got him married with the hope that his ways would change. Old habits die hard. Not only did Kashinath not change, but also a few months after marriage he ran away from home (in the Dhulia district of Maharashtra), leaving a departing note and reached Nasik. However, two months later, anxiety about the plight of his parents compelled him to return home. Shortly thereafter his wife expired, but before the cup of sorrow could be emptied, Kashinath, now fifteen, was married off a second time. To earn his livelihood he went to places like Pune, but could not find a job because of the absence of any formal education. At times he did menial work for others and at other times, he took to begging. He was in a miserable state. Sometimes, he even had to sleep on footpaths (sidewalks) and live only on Margosa (*neem*) leaves.

During this period of trials and tribulations, he met a saint who impressed upon him the virtues of *Brahmacharya* (celibacy). Leaving Pune he went to a place called Kalyan, where he resorted to begging as a means of livelihood, often quenching his hunger only by drinking water. A few days later, frustrated and exhausted, he decided to return home. He reached home in July 1890. Soon after, his father passed away. To earn his livelihood, he practised medicine for some time, followed by the job of a *Malgujari* (tax collector for the king or ruler). However, he failed in all the material ventures he undertook. His health also deteriorated substantially due to neglect and lack of comforts. While practising *pranayama* (breath control exercises), his breath-cycle also got disturbed.

Even his sleep, digestion and eliminatory systems were affected. All medical and religious efforts having failed, he tried to get occult help from a *Yogi*. A Yogi called Yogi Kulkarni whom Kashinath met at Rahuri, told him that he had entered a high *yogic* state and therefore, must take the help of Shri Sai Baba of Shirdi. Presuming Shri Sai to be a Muslim, Kashinath did not take the advice seriously. One day when Kashinath was walking in the streets of Rahuri, an old man approached him and advised him to drink hot water as a curative measure and to avoid drinking cold water. Kashinath did not take this unsolicited advice given by an unknown person, but continued his search for a Hindu *Yogi*. While on this search, at a certain place called Jajuri, he went into a *Samadhi* state while sitting in a lonely place surrounded by a prickly-pear bush. When he awoke, he felt very thirsty and went to the stream nearby to drink water. At that time the same old man reappeared from nowhere. He repeated his advice in an angry tone and disappeared suddenly. Kashinath took his advice (this time) seriously and found immediate relief. In a short time his health became all right by this hot-water therapy. Then he went to meet Narayan Maharaj of Kedgaon, a famous saint. On his way back he again met Yogi Kulkarni at Rahuri, who once again insisted that he should meet Sai Baba, as Shirdi was on the way. Ultimately Kashinath came to Shirdi and met Shri Sai on 27th June 1911. Little did he realise at that time that he had met his *Sadguru* (Master) and that the course of his life would undergo a complete transformation thereafter.

After staying at Shirdi for about two or three days, Kashinath wanted to leave for home. Obviously he had been wishing for a happy reunion with his family members and hoped to live with them happily ever after. However, Sai would not agree. Everyone in Shirdi knew that if Shri Sai did not permit one to leave Shirdi, there must be something more to it. Those who disobeyed faced problems, which could have been avoided, had they heeded the words of Shri Sai. When Kashinath pleaded vehemently, Shri Sai ultimately permitted him on the condition that he (Kashinath) should return to Shirdi in eight days. Kashinath, not having full faith in Sai yet, started worrying and fretting as eight days was too short a time. Sai, knowing his mental state told him, "Well, go if you like, I will see what can I do." Very happy at the prospect of going home, he made a quick departure. However, strangely enough, moving from place to place, he reached Kopergaon (a village 8 miles away from Shirdi) on the eighth day. He was utterly confused and did not know how, in eight days of continuous walking, he could only cover eight miles. Willy-nilly from Kopergaon, he came to Shirdi with a group of pilgrims and met Shri Sai again.

When he bowed before Shri Sai, the latter spoke to him.

Sai : "So you have come. When did you leave this place?"

Kashinath : "Thursday."

Sai : " At what time?"

Kashinath : "At three."

Sai : "What day of the week is this?"

Kashinath : "Thursday."

Sai : "How long since you left?"

Kashinath : "A week. Today is the eighth day."

Sai : "That's it. When you left, you protested that you could not return within eight days!"

Kashinath : "I do not know how this has happened. It is all your doing."

Sai : "Man, I was behind you all these eight days. Now go and stay in that *wada* (i.e. Kaka Saheb's, where visitors of Shri Sai usually stayed. *Wada* means a building within a compound).

From that day onwards, Kashinath was put on probation by Shri Sai, who asked him to stay in the *wada* (a place where the other pilgrims were staying). Kashinath attempted to understand more about Sai by enquiring about Him from other devotees and observing His daily activities. One day, Sai as usual narrated a peculiar story in the form of a self-experience to the assembled devotees. He said that once He met an emaciated and pregnant woman, whom He advised to drink only hot water and avoid cold water, so that the child could be delivered early. She did not heed His advice but went on drinking cold water. He again came and advised the lady not to take cold water but to take hot water only. When she started to take hot water, she delivered the child. While narrating the story Shri Sai pointed frequently at Kashinath, who was convinced that it was Shri Sai who had appeared at two places to save him. Love and gratitude engulfed him so much that he started crying. Sai told him clearly that He and Kashinath had *Rinanubandha* (*karmic* obligations of the past, including the previous births) for many centuries.

To protect Kashinath from all external factors that affect spiritual growth, Sai asked him to go and sit in the Khandoba Temple and do nothing, so that Sai would be able to do whatever He wished to do i.e. to work within Kashinath and evolve him. Sai told Kashinath that Khandoba's (Lord Shiva's) full grace would come on him after a period of four years.

Like a mother protecting its child from the onslaughts of nature and of people around, even at the cost of her own life, Shri Sai protected Kashinath wholeheartedly and openly. Before the assemblage of jealous devotees, who asked the reason for His extreme grace, He said, "Yes, yes, everything has been given, whatever he is, good or bad, he is mine. There is no distinction between him and me. Now, the whole responsibility for him rests with me." Kashinath still could not understand the import of the words of Shri Sai. To further indicate his future, Sai said "Wherever you are, you are God – you will realise everything."

The grace of the *Sadguru* is immeasurable. The *Sadguru* is responsible for everything, good or evil, done by the pupil. At this stage, the *Sadguru* virtually remains at the mercy of the disciple. By this total sacrifice of Himself, the *Sadguru* evolves the disciple to a state of perfection, i.e. His own state. Shri Sai once told one of His close associates that the endeavour should be to create these perfect men so that they can, in turn, spiritually uplift thousands and millions of other souls from the state of *Jivatma* (bonded souls) to the state of *Shivatma* (perfect souls). To evolve Kashinath was no easy task for Shri Sai. It is said that the difference in the state of consciousness between a stone and an ordinary man is the difference between an ordinary man and a *Sadguru*. Like a man turning a piece of stone by the use of hammer and chisel into a beautiful piece of sculpture, the *Sadguru* can change a gross individual to a perfect soul. This is what Shri Sai was trying to do with Kashinath. The methods He used were, sometimes, harsh from the point of view of Kashinath, but, none the less were meant for his evolution to that perfect state.

To begin His work, Sai told Kashinath "Sit quiet, somehow. Have nothing to do with anyone." Sai wanted Kashinath not to create further *samskaras* or impressions for himself by attachment with other people, but to draw his mind inwards. As he followed the master, a series of mystic reactions happened in Kashinath and around him.

To make Kashinath realise that his *Guru* (Shri Sai) was present in every living being irrespective of the species, He once told Kashinath that He would one day visit Khandoba temple (where Kashinath used to stay). He wondered whether

Kashinath would recognise Him. About two or three months later Kashinath was taking some food to his *Guru,* who was sitting at the Dwarkamayee mosque. A black dog who had been watching Kashinath while cooking, followed him. Without giving any food to the dog, Kashinath went straight to Sai, who said, "Why did you take the trouble to bring the food here, in this hot sun? I was sitting there (i.e. near the temple)." Kashinath was shocked to hear that his *Guru* was at the temple and he did not know. He told Sai that there was no one in the temple except a black dog. At that, Sai said "Yes, yes, I was that dog." Hearing this, Kashinath could not stop crying and resolved never again to commit such a blunder. The next day, while cooking, he looked around cautiously lest the dog came again. The dog was nowhere to be seen. A *Shudra* (lower-caste) beggar was leaning against a wall and watching him cook. Kashinath the *Brahmin* (uppermost caste), reared in the orthodox tradition, immediately asked him to go away. Later when he approached Sai, the latter told him "Yesterday you did not give me food and today also you ordered me not to stand there and drove me away. Do not bring food for me hereafter." Again Kashinath was surprised and again he was told that the *shudra* was Sai Himself. These two lessons taught Kashinath that God and Shri Sai are in everything, and that the essence of God pervades everyone and everything.

On the *Gurupurnima* day (*Ashadha* full moon day) of 1913, Shri Sai asked a devotee Chandrabai, a strong-willed lady to worship Kashinath the way Sai was being worshipped. This lady approached Kashinath in Khandoba temple with the *Pooja* (worship) materials. Kashinath refused to be worshipped and even threatened her for her audacious act. But Chandrabai told him (in the language of Sai) that even his body, which he thought was being worshipped, did not belong to him. From this day onwards Kashinath was called Upasani Maharaj, since officially Sai installed him as a *Guru* even in his probation period. After this incident, he started losing consciousness of his body (*Dehabhava*).

Now Upasani Maharaj started having visions and feelings of a highly psychic and spiritual nature. For example, he lost his normal vision by looking at the sun constantly. The sun and other light sources looked dark to him. When in this state, one day, he suddenly started seeing circles of light, which expanded and then came near him. These circular specks of light would disappear on coming near his body. Now he started seeing spiritual visions inside these circles of light. One day he saw himself standing at some place in the space and saw the whole cosmos including the sun, moon and sky revolving. The whirling cosmos slowly became smaller and smaller, came towards him, and vanished near him or into him. Upasani Maharaj now began to realise that the whole world was illusory and revolving and that he, as a soul, was outside it. This was a higher stage in his spiritual growth.

From his childhood Upasani Maharaj had identified the body as the cause of all evils in life and had made conscious attempts to punish it. For a spiritual aspirant, identifying the body with the self is a big limitation. How Shri Sai removed this limitation is an interesting story. One day Upasani Maharaj saw a vision that in an old building he (Upasani) and Sai were there. Shri Sai beckoned him to bring his ear close to His (Sai's) mouth so that He could give him a mantra. When Upasani Maharaj tried to do so, a shabby figure, which looked exactly like him tried to pull Maharaj away from Sai. Then Sai beat up that shabby figure, carried him out and burnt him in a pyre. Identifying himself with this figure, when Upasani complained about this action (of burning), Shri Sai told him that it was his (Maharaj's) evil form, which had been burnt. A little later, he saw an illuminated figure of himself. Again on being asked, Sai said that it was his (Maharaj's) virtuous form. Maharaj was surprised and asked that if he had an evil form and also a virtuous form, then who was he! Shri Sai told him that he was beyond both these forms and was the pure soul, the element of which Shri Sai Himself was made.

As Upasani Maharaj proceeded from the stage of illumination to self-realisation, occult powers and *siddhis* came to him. When an aspirant evolves in the spiritual path, higher psychic and occult powers gradually grow in him. He could read the minds of everyone — his past, present and future. People started surrounding him and he had a substantial following.

Often, when he was being worshipped by a few persons, a crazy ascetic called Nanavali, who stayed at Shirdi, would come and pull out his cloth and talk to him with disrespect and contempt. Once he tied him and beat him up. As Nanavali was a tough and dangerous person, no one could protect Upasani Maharaj. His cup of sorrow was full, but inwardly his Godly qualities were evolving to perfection. He was getting ready for his new and bigger role. Every time he faced a problem, Sai assured him by saying that He (Sai) was always with him and that the more he suffered at present, the better it would be for his future.

One night in July 1914, Upasani Maharaj left Shirdi quietly, taking mental permission from his *Guru*, for a role he was destined to play elsewhere. First he went to a place called Shindi, then to Nagpur, where he stayed for about a month and finally, to Kharagpur. At all these places, people started worshipping him, even when he tried fervently to run away from such situations. He tried to remain incognito, but people would not leave him in peace. At Kharagpur, he deliberately stayed in a dirty condition and used filthy articles and even abused people in most unparliamentary language. People followed him everywhere and conducted his *Pooja* (worship) and demanded advice from him. When a flower blooms and its aroma spreads, butterflies and insects naturally get drawn towards it.

Same was the case with Upasani Maharaj. Since he had become a *Satpurush* (Perfect One) people naturally flocked to him, whether he liked it or not. All persons coming in contact with a *Satpurush* get purified. His following increased every day and his surroundings became a place for activities like feeding of the poor, *kirtan* and *Naamjap* (remembrance of the holy name, etc.) Although Upasani Maharaj was reluctant to display his powers, a number of miracles started happening around him. After staying for about a year in Kharagpur, when people tried to build a permanent abode for him, he quickly left the place. Soon he reached Nagpur, where also people surrounded him to have his *darshan*. After two months at Nagpur, he visited places like Pune and also his home at Satana. As his four-year period was over, he returned to Shirdi and stayed at the Khandoba temple for about seven months. Thereafter, he left for a place called Rahata where he conducted *naamjaps*, feeding of the poor, etc. From there he went to Ahmedabad for some time. Returning to Shirdi a third time, he stayed near his *Guru* for about two to three months. In 1917, he finally shifted to Sakori and started functioning as a spiritual master (*Sadguru*).

This child of Shri Sai served thousands and thousands of people, day in and day out with least regard for his personal comforts, and finally left his gross body in the early hours of the 24th day of December, in the year 1941. Like his *Guru*, Upasani Maharaj had given enough indications about his final departure earlier. Upasani Maharaj was Shri Sai's loftiest creation: a stone turned into a touchstone. When one goes through the dramatically episodic life of Upasani Maharaj and its culmination at the point of divinity, by the grace of his *Guru*, the question arises "Who is Sainath then? How should we measure Him? Can we really? Let us not try. Let us surrender to Him, for He is the Ultimate!"

Glossary

Aarti - Prayer performed with lighted lamps, etc.
Ananta - One who has no end
Anantagarba- Divine core
Adi Purusha - the original state of God
Adharma - Non-righteousness
Ahetuk Kripa - un-qualified divine grace
Asnas - Yogic and meditative postures
Ashada - Monsoon month in the Hindu calendar
Advaita - a philosophy that preaches Monism
Bhakti - devotion
Bhakt - devotee
Brahmistha/Paramahamsa - a God realised state
Brahma - The creator of the universe
Bhakti yoga - The path of devotion
Chilium - Indian clay pipe for smoking
Chapati - Indian home-made bread
Darshan - to get an audience/meeting
Dhuni - the sacred fire
Dakshina - money given as an offering
Dhyan Yoga - the method of concentration/meditation
Dharma - Righteousness
Dhristhi Diksha - spiritual empowerment through looks
Daya nidhi - the ocean of compassion
Durachara - unrighteous behaviour
Dehabhawa - sense of body or ego of body
Dusshera - An Indian festival
Dherand Samhita - A holy book written by Dherand Rishi
Gorakh Samhita - A holy book written by Sadguru Gorakhnath ji

Grihasta - A family man

Ganapati - Elephant God, son of Shiva and Parvati

Guru Poornima - Indian Festival, day of Guru worship

Gita - Spiritual discourse in Mahabharat - The epic
Krishna to Arjuna

Guna - qualities

Gossains - term of address for God, Devas and spiritual people.

Gyana - Wisdom

Hiranyagarbha - cosmic egg

Hatha Yoga - a kind of Yoga or exercise

Halwa - Indian sweet

Hazur - reverential address e.g. 'sir'

Iti - as it is or end

Ishwar Chetana - God consciousness

Ishwar tatwa - God elements or theories

Jagirdar - Landlord

Jeewan-mukta- one who is free from the cycles of birth and death

Jiva- soul

Jamun- blackberry

Jivatma- living forms

Jyoti- light

Karma- actions

Kheer - Indian sweet made of milk and sugar

Kafni - A long shirt

Kirtan - devotional songs and music

Kriyasheel Brahma - God in active or manifested form

Kriya Yoga- a yogic path

Kazi - Judge

Kripa Sindhu - Ocean of compassion

Kalpavriksha - the wish-fulfilling tree

Langar - free distribution of food to the poor and needy

Leela - Divine miracles

Laddoo - Indian sweets.

Mahesh- Another name for Shiva

Mahasamadhi - The entombment of saints

Maha Shivaratri - An Indian festival of Shiva worship

Maulvi - Muslim priest
Maya - worldly illusion
Madarsa - Muslim religious school
Mantra - religious verses having spiritual-occult potentiality
Moharram - Muslim festival, of Prophet Muhammed
Mahayana - A branch of Buddhism
Natha - God or husband or saint
Narayana - The Preserver or Vishnu
Nad Brahma - Cosmic Sound
Navnatha - The nine saints or the Natha cult
Namaz - The Islamic prayers
Naamjap - non-stop chanting of the Lord's name
Naivedya -- offering to the Lord
Omkar - The primordial sound of creation 'Om' or 'Aum'
Pooja - Hindu worship
Parayana - reading of Hindu religious books
Prasad - distribution of the offering made to the Lord
Param Sadguru - the chief among the Sadgurus
Param Yogins - the realised yogis
Pranayam - Breath controlling exercises
Param brahma - the ultimate creator
Prakriti- Nature
Panchbooth - the five basic elements of nature
Puja vidhi - methods of worship
Puranas - Ancient Hindu scriptures
Pandit - Priest or learned person
Paduka - Footwear of the Lord or Guru
Peda - Indian sweet
Puri - Indian bread, fried in oil
Punya- merits of good deeds
Pragyan Rithambhara - Power to know the past and future and
      more
Rudra Puran - an ancient Hindu scriputure
Raja Yoga- a royal path for a spiritual seekers
Ram Navami - Birthday of Lord Rama
Risaldar - one who grooms horses

Rinaunubandha- Karmic relationship over several births
Sainaam - chanting of the name of Shri Sai.
Sidha - possessor of occult-spiritual powers
Shastra - Hindu scriptures
Sankalp - on oath
Shakti - Goddess of Power or forces of nature
Seshnag - The king of snakes - the unmanifested power or creator
Satyanarayana - Lord Vishnu
Samarth Guru - a Guru having supernatural powers
Sadhu - one who has given up all wordly pursuits, mendicant
Shakti Pat - transfer of power from Guru to disciple
Swechchachara - one who moves of his own free volition.
Shivatma- the purest soul.
Samadhi - the place where a holy person is laid to rest.
Tejo Megh - highly charged energy fields emanating out of the
     cosmic egg after the big-bang
Tantra - Occultism
Tulsi - Basil
Tazia - carried by muslims in procession
Tandava Nritya- Cosmic Dance of Lord Shiva
Turiya - a high stage of spiritual development
Udi - the ashes from the sacred fire.
Upanishads- Hindu religious scriptures
Vedas - Hindu religious scriptures
Vishnu - The sustaining power of creation
Vishnu Puran - A Hindu scripture
Videha - sense of body's non-existence.
Vyom - sky
Wadas - Places of stay for guests.

C. B. Satpathy, a celebrated IPS Officer, is an ardent
devotee of Shirdi Sai Baba. He came into contact with
Shirdi Sai Baba in 1991 and since then has been
instrumental in publishing a range of literature, producing
music and building temples that are dedicated to
Sai philosophy.

He lives in Delhi, is married and has three children.